Twelve Miracles
Including
A Glimpse of Heaven

By
Nellie K. Hartsoe

Copyright © 2013 by Nellie K. Hartsoe

Twelve Miracles Including a Glimpse of Heaven
by Nellie K. Hartsoe

Printed in the United States of America

ISBN 9781625096845

All rights reserved solely by the author. The author guarantees all contents are original and do not infringe upon the legal rights of any other person or work. No part of this book may be reproduced in any form without the permission of the author. The views expressed in this book are not necessarily those of the publisher.

Unless otherwise indicated, Bible quotations are taken from The King James Version.

www.xulonpress.com

"And he gave some, apostles; and some, prophets; and some, evangelists; and some, pastors and teachers;"
Ephesians 4:11

God gives each one of us special gifts. I believe He blessed me with the ability to teach and touch lives adding, not only knowledge for professional use, but knowledge to enhance their spiritual life. I am grateful for the opportunity to share His love and wisdom with a multitude of students during the past 50 years.

Students' comments about Nellie K. Hartsoe as a professional educator. Comments were made anonymously during the Fall semester 2012.

Mrs. Hartsoe is always available for help.

Mrs. Hartsoe was thorough with her teaching. When grading assignments she writes revisions in that will help me gain more knowledge about the subject.

She is very informative, she provides very helpful information. She is interesting and always has a good life lesson to teach as well.

Mrs. Hartsoe is a great English teacher and I enjoyed her class and teaching style.

I love the teacher. She was amazing. She's another reason why I am pursuing my major in Education.

She went above and beyond what she needed to, to help someone in need!

Always came to class prepared and ready to teach. Helped every student and always gave positive feedback and was very nice to every student.

She is one of the best instructors I have had and I hope to have her next semester.

She's the best teacher I have ever had. May God bless her.

Mrs. Hartsoe has been my oldest instructor, however, her methods of teaching has been the best since I have attended this school.

She gives assignments that make you think for yourself instead of just conforming to society. I really enjoy her personal stories of faith and life.

Mrs. Hartsoe is a caring teacher and she wants to see all her students learn. She is a strong motivator. I never liked English before this semester now I love it.

INTRODUCTION And SPECIAL THANKS

During the year it has taken me to write this book, there were several interruptions. It was difficult to talk about some of the situations and I had to stop, cry, recoup, pray harder, thank God, and then some time later continue the task of completing what so many through the years have asked me to do, **Write the book.** James, my first grandchild's comments were probably the most influential in my decision to write the book. He kept telling me how he shared some of my experiences with friends and it had made a difference in their lives. As we ate breakfast every Sunday morning following the early morning worship service (he plays and sings in the praise band and then we go out for breakfast) he would tell me about an incident where he had shared some of my experiences and blessings from God with someone and then he would urge me to write the book. Sometimes I would share one of my experiences with my students when it related to what we were studying about and many of their comments included, "You need to write a book." So, I have finally written the book. April 10, 2013 will be the 59th anniversary of the accident that led to my being pronounced DOA (Dead on Arrival). You will see how and why this was a miracle as you read the book.

I want to thank the following people for their assistance throughout my life.

Immeasurable Assistance in writing and editing this book.

James (Jimmy) – my first grandchild

Karen Jeglum Kennedy – sister-in-law(30+ years) Partner Gene Kennedy Enterprises

Faye Seyle – sister (with me for 69 of my 77 years)

My children – Jerry Jr. (Buzzy), Terri, and Steven

Others who had a positive impact on my life.

My Mother and Father

My brothers: Leroy Kennedy, Jr., and Kenneth Gene Kennedy

My sister-in-law Mary Lou Kennedy, married to my oldest brother for 60 years and has shared the past 62 years with me as my friend.

A special tribute and thanks for sharing most of the miracles in my life and loving me unconditionally for almost 52 years. My loving husband Jerry E. Hartsoe

Nellie is a motivational speaker and available for speaking engagements.

You may contact her by Email NKHartsoe@aol.com

TABLE OF CONTENTS

Chapter One:

    The First Miracle - The Miracle of Birth 11

Chapter Two:

    The Early Years 14

Chapter Three:

    The Second Miracle - Learning to walk again
at age 10 22

Chapter Four:

    The Third Miracle – An accident saved my foot 27

Chapter Five:

    The Fourth Miracle - Meeting the Love of My Life 44

Chapter Six:

    The Fifth Miracle – Out of Body Experience 72

Chapter Seven:

    The Sixth Miracle - Starting our Family 105

Chapter Eight:

    The Seventh Miracle -Stroke: Learning to Walk
Again at age 38 152

Chapter Nine:
    The Eighth Miracle - Walking without a Brace 155
Chapter Ten:
    The Ninth Miracle – Creative Ministries 172
Chapter Eleven:
    The Tenth Miracle - Life Without Jerry 175
Chapter Twelve:
    The Eleventh Miracle –Learning to walk again
    at age 72 202
Chapter Thirteen:
    The Twelfth Miracle - Learning to walk again
    at age 76 207
Chapter Fourteen:
    The Story Continues 212

Chapter One:

The first miracle. My birth.

"... *Whosoever shall not receive the kingdom of God as a little child, he shall not enter therein. And he took them up in his arms, put his hands upon them and blessed them.*"

Mark 10:16

At the stroke of midnight a baby was born. That baby was me, Nellie. Since my birth was at midnight, the doctor asked my mother if she wanted my birth date to be recorded as the 18th or 19th of the month. My mother's labor had been on the 18th so she said, " make it the 18th." So, my official birth certificate reads – baby girl – born to Janie Modean Haselden Kennedy and Le Roy Kennedy – 18th September, 1935. My birth is the first miracle. You'll have to read on to find out why I consider it the first miracle God has given me.

I have to stop here and tell you a little about my mother and father. My father was twenty-one years old and a mail carrier with his own car (that was a luxury in 1929). My mother was fourteen.

Her sister's boyfriend was friends with my father and had told him about my mother. My father drove past my mother's home and saw her outside playing with her brothers and sisters (mother was the middle child of thirteen children). He didn't stop, but went home and told his mother that he had just seen the girl he was going to marry. He convinced her sister's boyfriend (Curvin) to get my mother to go out with them and he would tag along. They did this and on that date my father also convinced Curvin to go to the justice of the peace and marry Mary (mother's sister) so he could marry my mother. They agreed and proceeded to the justice of the peace (marriage licenses were issued at the time, they didn't have to wait like you have to do today) and on Sept. 11, 1930 my mother and father were married. My oldest brother (Leroy, Jr.) was born October 25, 1931 and my other brother (Kenneth Gene) was born October 3, 1933.

LeRoy, Jr. Nellie, Gene

Since I wasn't born until 1935, I'm relating this from what my mother told me. My father was a rounder in their early days of marriage and he also drank and smoked. Often times my mother and brothers would stay with my grandparents while my father did his "thing." After I was born things changed somewhat.

Mother had been in labor all day and finally Daddy came home early evening and my mother asked him to

The first miracle. My birth.

go get the doctor. Daddy left, picked up a couple of girls and didn't come back until the next day. A neighbor went for the doctor and by the time he arrived I was coming breech birth – feet first – and to save my mother's life and mine the doctor literally pulled me from my mother by my right leg. In the process he tore all the ligaments in my right side leaving me with a bulge in my right side that remained until I had major surgery when I was ten to correct it. Mother said that the doctor, with God's help, saved her life and mine and that is why I consider my birth the first miracle God gave me.

When my father returned the next morning and realized what he had done, he changed his lifestyle and became a supportive, faithful husband and father. In fact, I don't ever remember a time when I saw my father (or mother) drink, smoke or use bad language.

Chapter Two:

The Early Years.

"Train up a child in the way he should go: and when he is old, he will not depart from it." Proverbs 22:6

My mother is very creative and she had prayed for a little girl so she could make pretty dresses for her. She did just that and I was one of the best dressed babies in the community. You might say I was spoiled. I was a smart little girl and because of my birth injury I couldn't run and play like other children so I learned every song on the radio and I would sing and dance and perform for anybody who would watch me. We lived in a rural area and there was only a small school. When I was four years old, the principal came to mother and asked her to let me go to first grade (pre-school didn't exist at that time) because they needed one more child to keep the teacher they had. She said it didn't matter if I couldn't do the work, I could always repeat the grade the next year. Mother agreed and so I started regular school in the first grade at the age of 4. In fact, school started in August and I turned 4 on Sept. 18, 1939. I loved school and I

The Early Years.

passed all the tests and out read all the other kids and to the surprise of everyone, I was promoted to second grade at the ripe old age of five.

My fifth year in this world was an unusual year. A talent contest was held and my mother entered me in it. I sang and danced and won the competition. The promoters of the contest wanted me to go to Hollywood for a screen test. My mother only had a 4th grade education and was scared of all their talk and promises and refused to let me go or to go with me so my chance for stardom was lost. Also that year I received the only two spankings I have ever had from my mother (my father never spanked us; he would talk us to death and make us feel so bad that we never wanted to disappoint him ever again). Believe it or not the spankings resulted from my acting and singing abilities.

In those days, the Salvation Army had a band and would stand on the street and play and sing as people dropped coins in their red kettles. On this particular day, mother and I had gone shopping and I spotted the band and wanted to go across the street so I could dance and sing with them, but mother had other ideas and refused to go, so I pulled my hand from hers and proceeded to cross the busy street and get right up in front of everyone and started doing "my thing". Everyone thought I was the cutest thing – everyone, except my mother, of course, who interrupted my performance by taking me to the side and applying the hand of education to the seat of understanding.

Several weeks later my mother was singing in the church choir and they always sat in the front of the church. She would park me with a relative or friend on a pew in the congregation. On this particular Sunday, several of the teenagers convinced me to sit with them. I was extremely proud that they wanted me to sit with them in the "back of the church". I truly didn't know that teenagers try to get little children in trouble so they can laugh at them. They knew I knew all of the hit songs and while the preacher was preaching they persuaded me to sing a song for them. I was flattered and all I knew was I was being asked to sing and I loved to sing. I started out singing – now singing in church should have been o.k. - Only problem was –the preacher was preaching and I didn't sing a church song. I sang, "Down in the meadow in the little bitty pool swam three little fishes and the mama fish too. Swim said the moma fish, swim if you can and they swam and they swam all over the dam, dam, dam . . ." That's as far as I got because at that point, my mother grabbed my hand and marched me outside and again applied the hand of education to the seat of understanding. How she could move that fast to get up from the front of the church and get to the back of the church without my knowing it, I still don't understand. I guess God gives mother's extra energy when their offspring misbehaves.

When I was six and in the third grade, my father received a promotion and we moved from Florence, SC to Charleston, SC and he went to work for the newspaper. He drove a truck and delivered newspapers throughout South Carolina. The newspaper company wanted him so badly that they also provided a place for us to live. It was the most unusual place and we (my brother's and I) thought

The Early Years.

it was a great place to live. It had been a radio station and sat up on poles over part of the marsh. It was at the end of the street so there wasn't a lot of traffic. We would play in the marsh and throw rocks at the mud crabs. At that time we didn't realize that crabs were worth money and that people loved to eat them, especially crab legs. We just played with them. Once in a while if we weren't careful one of us would get pinched and it hurt. We were also only about 4 blocks from the city park and it was fun to go to the park and play games and swing on the swings.

We had to walk several blocks to school. I always loved school and the new school was exciting and I met many new friends. I was a pretty good student in school. I didn't have to study very much and I always made good grades.

I enjoyed being the only girl in my family and I admit I was spoiled rotten. My mother still sat me up on the table and put my socks (with lace trim around the top) and shoes on when I was in the fourth grade. My brothers always treated me special. I was tiny and petite at that time – not big as a minute – as the saying goes and my brothers were my protectors.

We didn't get toys or candy every time we went to the store. Daddy made a good living, but the Second World War had started and everything was rationed. Moma could only get a little sugar, rice, flour and other things. She always found enough money to buy material and trim to sew and make my pretty dresses. Christmas, Easter, and birthdays were special. I want to tell you about them.

Easter was a time for focusing on the crucifixion and resurrection of Jesus. Even though we got an Easter basket and had an egg hunt, Moma never let us forget that the real celebration was for Jesus because He had given His life for our sins. The other things I remember so clearly about Easter was that I always got a new dress, socks, shoes, gloves, and hat. My brothers always got a new suit, shirt, tie, socks and shoes. Moma, of course, made mine and everything matched, even the gloves I had to wear.

Christmas time was a time for secrets. Packages hid here and there and Moma was always sewing and hiding what she made. Christmas was also a time for remembering that it was Jesus' birthday and He was the reason for our giving gifts because He was the greatest gift ever given. God loved us so much that He sent His only Son so all who believed could be saved.

At Christmas, we would have a Christmas tree and a lot of the decorations were homemade but we enjoyed making them. We didn't have stockings back then like they do now, but we would put a shoe box in front of the fireplace for Santa to leave our "goodies".

Every year we would get an apple, an orange, a banana, stick candy, some nuts and raisins in our shoe boxes. My brothers would get a new gun and holster set, a cowboy hat, and a stick horse. I would get new doll clothes for my special doll, a tea set, and a new dress. However, before we could even touch our gifts, we had to sit around in our pajamas and daddy would read the Christmas story and we would blow out the candles on the cake Moma had made for Jesus'

The Early Years.

birthday and sing happy birthday to Jesus. Then we would feast on hoecakes, chocolate to sop, and bacon. We had hot chocolate with marshmallows. Then we could go and play with our new things. As I said, Christmas was a happy, joyous time in our home.

The only other time we got anything extra was on our birthday. Moma always made us feel very special on our birthday. There was a cake, ice cream, and friends to share it with.

If we were poor, we never knew it because Moma and Daddy always made sure we had what we needed and they always shared with some of my other relatives. We especially shared with Moma's family. A couple of her brothers had several children and their jobs didn't pay much so Moma would give my clothes and my brother's clothes that we had outgrown to my cousins. Sometimes she would get angry with me because I wanted to give away some of my new clothes and some of the prettiest clothes to a special cousin I had. She asked me why was it important to me to give the best I had and I told her because I wanted Dean (a special cousin) to look pretty.

Moma and Daddy were Christians and we went to church every Sunday and Wednesday. One Sunday they made a plea for Sunday school teachers and I asked my mother to be our Sunday school teacher. She said she was afraid to do that because she only had a fourth grade education and might not be able to pronounce some of the words and she would be embarrassed. Since I was in the fourth grade, I promised I would help her and we would study before Sunday and if there were words we couldn't pronounce I would take it to school and get my school teacher to tell me the word and then I would tell it to Moma so she wouldn't have to be embarrassed. With that understanding, she volunteered to teach my Sunday school class. I was so proud to have my Moma teaching my class.

Life was going along pretty well. Then I got a surprise and a shock the Christmas I was in the fifth grade. When I was a child sex was not a subject that was openly discussed. So when my mother began gaining weight I didn't even notice. Then one day in December – just a week before Christmas - Moma got very sick. It was snowing (which was unusual) and it snowed so hard the ambulance couldn't get to our house so my father and a friend carried my mother a block to the ambulance. I was really scared. Moma had never been sick, not like this. The next morning Daddy told us we had a new little sister. Moma had had a baby – and it was a girl. Wow! I was happy and I was unhappy. I asked Daddy if I could pick out the baby's name and he said o.k. I thought about all kinds of names and none of them seemed good enough for my baby sister. After two days of thinking and thinking I finally came up with a name. I wanted to name her Kathryn Kate Kennedy. When Daddy came home I told him the name I wanted to name her and he said I was too late. They had already named her Carolyn Faye Kennedy. I was disappointed, but Moma said Kathryn Kate Kennedy would not have been a good name because it was during segregation and the Klu Klux Klan was very active and her initials would have been the same as theirs if her name was Kathryn Kate Kennedy. So I said it was o.k. to name her Carolyn

The Early Years.

Faye Kennedy. She was so squiggly and little. I loved playing with her, but I was also jealous of her because she took up so much of Moma's time. My brothers just acted like it didn't matter. They had wanted a boy so he could play cowboys and Indians with them.

Chapter Three:

The Second Miracle.
Learning to walk again at age 10

"Have mercy upon me, O Lord; for I am weak: O Lord, heal me; for my bones are vexed."

Psalm 6:2

I was 10 years old and in the sixth grade - and I had a boyfriend. He would walk me home and carry my books for me. His name was Ernest. I had several close girlfriends and my house was the gathering place. Moma made our home everyone's home and my friends enjoyed coming to my house. Moma was a stay at home mom and she always had Johnny cakes (large cookies baked on top of the stove, not in the oven) or something to snack on and made everyone welcome in our home.

The summer between my sixth and seventh grade brought a new experience for me. My parents decided it was time to "fix" my birth defect. I was to have surgery to repair the damage done to my right side when I was born. It had gotten so much worse. I still could not run and play like other kids. I continued to occupy my time listening to records and the radio (we didn't have TV – it didn't exist at that time). I would make up dances, and act and put on programs. I loved it when others would clap at my "performances". We went to church, I knew about God and Jesus, but I didn't know how to accept Him as my Savior. My mom and dad wanted me baptized before I had surgery – I guess they thought that would protect me and since I went to church regularly and read the Bible they thought I understood and so I was baptized when I was 10 years old.

Roper Hospital had just been completed and I was one of the first people to have surgery in the new surgery wing of the hospital. I was really scared.

My daddy had had his appendix out and he told me not to be afraid. I would just go to sleep and when I woke up it would be all over and I wouldn't feel anything. He also told me that when they were putting him to sleep with ether they told him to open his mouth and breathe deep and he would go to sleep. While I was in the operating room and they were getting ready to put me to sleep, I remembered what daddy had said and I made up my mind that I was not going to open my mouth. I guess I felt that if I kept my mouth closed I wouldn't go to sleep and they wouldn't cut me open. The nurse was ready to put the mask over my face. I had my mouth closed tight. She asked me if I had a boyfriend and I opened my mouth to tell her yes and he was really cute and once I opened my mouth that was it. I never did get to tell her I had a boyfriend.

Daddy was right about one thing. When I woke up the operation was all over. He was not right about saying that I wouldn't feel anything. I was in a lot of pain and I couldn't walk or get out of bed. I had to lay so very straight and not sit up. After a week in the hospital I went home. I still couldn't walk, but I could sit up. My boyfriend, Ernest, came over every day and sat with me. The day I came home from the hospital Ernest came over and brought me a great big cardboard box. When I opened the box, I found a layer of comic books, then a layer of mounds, a layer of comic books, then a layer of Baby Ruth's, a layer of comic books, then a layer of Hershey bars, and in all there were 5 layers of comic books and five layers of different kinds of candy bars.

It was wonderful. We would sit together and read the comic books and eat candy. Ernest came everyday and we spent an awful lot of time together. When it was time for me to try to walk, he would help me. He would put his arm around my waist and I would take a few steps. This went on the entire summer. I actually remember that summer as one of the happiest times of my life. God had given me another miracle and through the experience and training of the doctors and nurses, my birth injury was corrected.

By the time school started I could walk without help. I still couldn't run and play as the surgery needed more time to heal from the inside out (at that time I didn't understand what that meant – but it brought me more attention and I liked that). Ernest would come by every morning and walk with me to school. He would carry my books for me. I felt so special.

Sometimes we do foolish things, not realizing when we are doing well. I was in the seventh grade and Ernest was still my boyfriend. However, it was at this time Beckman entered the picture. It happened at Ernest's twelfth birthday party. We were all playing games and I noticed that Beckman kept looking at me. I was flattered because Beckman was the captain of the football team and all the girls liked him. Ernest was a very mature, settled, brain and I was happy being his girlfriend, but something about Beckman interested me and so I paid a little more attention to him at the party than I did to Ernest. When it came time to go home, Ernest said he would walk me home.

Beckman said, "No way, she lives on my way home so I'll walk her home." So, I told Ernest he needed to stay and see his other guests home and he did. Well, needless to say, kids talk and Ernest didn't like being teased about Beckman stealing his girlfriend at his birthday party so we broke up. I might as well tell you that Beckman was a tease and in a week he was walking someone else home and I wound up walking home by myself. You see, Ernest never forgave me for embarrassing him that way and we never saw each other except at school and he would only nod if he saw me. Of course, I was crushed because now I didn't have a boyfriend.

My brothers and I looked forward to Saturdays. Daddy would give each one of us a quarter and we would catch the bus downtown and go to a movie. That quarter would pay for the bus ride to and from town, a ticket to the movie (which was usually a western and a serial that continued each week) a bag of popcorn, a drink and we even had a nickel left over to put into church and/or save in our piggy banks. One of the things our parents taught us to do was to tithe the money we were given or earned by doing chores. I have never stopped following that practice.

Chapter Four:

The third miracle. An accident and God saved my foot.

"I will both lay me down in peace, and sleep: for thou, Lord, only makest me dwell in safety."

Psalm 4:8

I had an accident the summer I was eleven. I was riding my bicycle and fell off the bicycle and my foot landed on a broken bottle (I was barefooted) and cut my left foot underneath my toes – almost cutting my toes off. I was rushed to the doctor and he sewed up my foot and put a bandage on it and told me to stay off of it so it could heal. Well, to make a long story short, I didn't stay off of it and while we were visiting friends, I decided to ride my friend's bicycle and fell off, landing on the injured foot breaking the stitches. Daddy rushed me to the quickest clinic closest to our friend's house and the doctor said it was a blessing that I broke the stitches because the foot had become infected and gangrene was beginning to set in and in a few days I would have become very ill and possibly lost my foot. God truly does look out for us even when we do foolish things. This accident (which I believe was a miracle from God) saved my foot.

The doctor had to completely reopen the wound, scrape it and stitch it up again and give me an antibiotic. Since it was a clinic they didn't have anything to give me to numb the foot and my mother and father took turns holding my leg still for the doctor to work. I think I developed strong vocal cords during this time. My mother said she walked almost a block away and could still hear my screams as the doctor reopened and scraped the infection away. Needless to say I didn't ride bicycles the rest of that summer as it took several weeks for the wound to heal and again I could only walk with crutches so the limited walking I had experienced the summer before when I had major surgery took place and my walking was again interrupted until the foot healed and by that time it was time to go back to school.

During this time I expanded on singing, acting, and putting on performances for my family and friends. I had started taking piano and voice lessons from Vernon Weston's School of Music. Our music director at church worked there and she was my teacher.

By the time I reached eighth grade we had moved to an apartment downtown and I had to change schools. For one year I attended Charleston High School. Here I was in a new school, having to meet new people, and I was at least one to two years younger than everybody else. During that year two things happened that I remember very well.

The third miracle. An accident and God saved my foot.

At the beginning of the year I took Home Economics which included learning how to sew and cook (mostly cookies). We also studied appearances and posture. We had a professional instructor of modeling come to class one day and each student had to walk across the room in front of everyone and the guest model instructor would critique us as far as our posture was concerned. At the time I was about 5 feet tall and weighed about 80 pounds. I am small boned and I was so skinny that my hip bones stuck out like a clothes hanger and I had to stuff my bra to even have any top at all. However, I thought I was really cute.

When I walked across the room I really strutted my stuff. Wow! Was I in for a rude awakening? The first words out of her mouth were—- "You walk like a duck! Your head sticks out in front and your twist makes your behind stick out just like a duck." The entire class just cracked up laughing. I was humiliated to the core. From that day on I was conscious of my posture. I really worked on walking with my head up high, not out front, and I tried really hard not to twist my behind.

Whatever I did must have helped, because the second thing I remember was being selected to be a part of the selection for King and Queen of Charleston High School. Only ninth through twelfth graders could be elected King or Queen and the boy and girl selected from each of the eighth grade classes made up the Court. Mother made me a beautiful pale green long formal dress. It was beautiful and I felt so honored to be a part of the Court. Especially after being told earlier in the year that I walked like a duck.

At the end of the year, my parents bought a house back in the area we had first lived in and I was back in school with all my friends. I was so happy. The house was beautiful and it had two stories. There were four bedrooms and my two brothers shared a room, my parents had a room, my sister had a room, and I had my very own room. Downstairs was a living room, dining room, kitchen and breakfast area. We had a big front porch, and a fenced back yard. When you walked inside the front door there on the left were the stairs to go upstairs and if you went straight ahead you would go into the breakfast room-kitchen. To the right of the stairs were glass doors called French doors leading into the living room which also had a beautiful fire place. We only had heat downstairs so we would have to hurry and get our baths (yes, in the cold), put our housecoats on and take our clothes and rush downstairs where it was nice and warm to put our clothes on. All of my high school days were spent in this home.

I learned a lot of lessons in this home. I really didn't have a lot of chores to do while growing up. I had to keep my room clean and wash the dishes after dinner on Sunday. I really didn't like doing dishes and yet, dishes taught me a valuable lesson. It seemed to me that doing dishes was beneath my dignity. My friends always had things planned on Sunday afternoon and many times I had to miss out or go late because there was no escaping the Sunday dishes. Sometimes it would take me all afternoon and that would put me in a terrible mood. I tried to make the best of it by practicing singing,

The third miracle. An accident and God saved my foot.

dancing and acting. The sink was on the back wall and had a window above it that looked out into the back yard. There was a mirror placed on the window sill and I would admire myself in the mirror, act out scenes from movies and plays, sing and dance all around the kitchen while doing the dishes. I always griped and complained about dishes taking up all my time on Sunday afternoon.

One Sunday afternoon I was busy singing, dancing, acting away, and oh, yes, doing the dishes and my mother walked in the kitchen and I started my griping and complaining about how I was missing out on the best times of my life doing the stupid dishes and they were just going to get dirty again and have to be washed again. It was a thankless job and robbed me of my time for pleasure and being with my friends.

My mother, very patiently said, "You are robbing yourself of pleasure time and yet, you are blaming the poor dishes for your poor judgment."

I said, "I am not. The dishes have to be done and you said it was my responsibility to do them—- ev-ev-ry Sunday so how am I robbing myself. You make me do the dishes."

My mother said, "You have six plates, six sets of silverware, six glasses, a couple of bowls, a couple of pots and a frying pan. If you applied yourself, you could wash the dishes in no more than 30 minutes and have plenty of time to do what you want to do. So, your singing, acting, dancing, entertaining yourself is robbing you of what you call 'pleasure time with your friends', not the dishes."

I didn't like what she said, but I had to admit that it made sense. I never learned to like washing dishes, but I did take my mother's advice and heeding that advice I realized that I had been robbing myself and not the dishes. That's a lesson I have applied to many situations throughout life. I may not enjoy something that I have to do, but if I apply myself, it can be done in a timely manner and leave time for other things I do enjoy doing.

My sister, Faye, always followed me around, but she was stubborn and wouldn't listen to me. You see, I was eight years older than her and I thought that gave me the right to boss her around. She, of course, felt she didn't have to listen to me. On one occasion Faye was playing in the back yard and mother told me to call her and tell her to come in for supper. Well, I called her, but instead of telling her that mother had said for her to come in for supper, I said, "Faye, get in this house for supper."

A little later, Faye was still playing in the back yard. Mother said, "Nellie, tell your sister she has five minutes to get in this house for supper."

I went to the back door and opened the screen door and yelled, "Carolyn Faye, Moma said you have five minutes to get in this house for supper."

Faye calmly put her hands on her hips and yelled back, "Well, let me know when the five minutes is up!"

She also had a habit of sitting in the living room when I had a boyfriend over. To get rid of her, my boyfriend would usually offer

The third miracle. An accident and God saved my foot.

---

her a nickel or dime and sometimes a quarter to leave us alone. She was happy to take the money and leave for a little while and then she would pop back in and stay put. Most of the time we got along well, and I guess I was a little bossy, but I loved having a little sister.

One of our next door neighbors had two children; Leonard, who was the same age as my brother that was two years older than me, and Linda, a girl my age. Leonard was really cute. Linda was nice and her bedroom window was right across from mine and we would often talk to each other across the driveway. Because I had two older brothers, nobody messed with me. If anybody said anything out of the way or bumped into me in the hallway, Gene and Jr. took care of it and it didn't happen anymore. I really feel that I was so lucky to have two older brothers who looked out for me. We didn't have a lot of trouble, but I always knew if I needed anything, they were there. They made me feel so special. Even after all this time, they still make me feel special.

Faye and Nellie

All during high school, I did the normal things. I was an office helper, grounds beautifier (I loved the times we were excused from class to plant pansies around the flag pole of Rivers High School), and part of the chorus (Gene was part of the chorus and he got his letter (Block R with a treble clef on it) to sew on his sweater after one year and I had to wait two years to get mine. When Gene received his letter and I didn't I asked the teacher why he got his and I didn't get mine and she said that I had a nice voice, but Gene had a God given voice so he deserved it after only one year and I would have to wait until next year for mine. Gene felt so bad that I didn't get my letter that he gave me his letter. Selfish me, I took it and put it on my sweater. I was also in the drama club and a cheerleader. I did manage to go to classes and keep my grades up in between all the extracurricular activities.

I didn't realize it at the time, but I was a snob and so were my friends. Something happened to help me be a better person. My friends and I would sit together for lunch in the cafeteria. There was a girl in our class that always sat by herself. She always wore shabby clothes and looked lost most of the time. In other words, she didn't fit in with us. We found out that her birthday was coming up and we decided to have some fun (I learned it isn't fun to make fun of someone) with her and so we pitched in and bought her a wash cloth, soap, deodorant, tooth brush and toothpaste. We wrapped it up carefully and invited her to sit with us at lunch. We sang happy birthday to her and gave her the "gift". She seemed so happy to be included with us and she unwrapped the present and when she saw what it was, she burst into tears and ran out of the cafeteria. We all laughed and laughed at the joke we had pulled on her. She didn't fit in anyway so what was the harm. We soon found out what harm it did. We were called to the principal's office and were asked why we did that. We told her that we were just joking. She asked us how well we

The third miracle. An accident and God saved my foot.

knew the girl and we told her we didn't know her because she didn't fit in with us and she was – just – different.

What the principal told us changed my attitude and made me want to be a better person that didn't judge or take advantage of other people. She told us that the girl lived with her old grandmother because her parents had been killed in a car accident. She said the girl had a younger brother and sister. She said the grandmother was in a wheelchair and couldn't do much in the way of taking care of the children and they were very poor since the only income they had was from welfare. She said the girl we took advantage of and treated so badly had to take care of the grandmother, brother, sister, do the laundry, cook, clean, and she wasn't any older than any of us. Our punishment for the way we treated the girl was to give up our recess time for a month and clean all the tables in the cafeteria and that while we were wiping tables to think about how we had behaved and find a way to tell the girl that we were sorry for what we had done.

We did just that and we asked her to forgive us and to be our friend. We helped get clothes for her and her brother and sister. We all learned a valuable lesson that day. The girl's name was Ann and she became one of my best friends. She spent many nights with me and I spent the night with her and helped her wash dishes, clean house, and help with whatever she needed me to do.

When I was in the tenth grade, I was fourteen and most of my classmates were fifteen and sixteen. Several of my friends worked in the local dime store. I told my mother I wanted to go to work. I always made good grades so she said I could as long as I kept my grades up. I applied for a job at Edward's Department Store. I passed the test and when Mr. Ed, the owner, interviewed me he told me that at fourteen I was too young. I said I am in the tenth grade and I'm on the honor roll and I passed your test. Mr. Ed told me to get a note from my principal concerning my grades and my parents giving permission and he would give me a chance.

At that time I did not know that this gentle giant of a man would play an important role in my life at a later time. He was Jewish and was over six feet tall with a big mustache. He also wore a built up shoe because he had polio as a child and it left one leg shorter than the other. Even though he was a large figure of a man, especially to me at 5 feet 90 pounds he was very gentle in his mannerism and showed that he really cared about people. I got a note from the principal and my parents and I went to work on the hosiery counter. Socks came packaged in boxes and had to be put in bins according to sizes.

Mary Lou and Nellie

I met Mary Lou at Edwards and we both worked on the hosiery counter. She went to a different school and she was my age, but she was in the right grade for her age – ninth – but we hit it off right away. For the next two years we did practically everything together. We

The third miracle. An accident and God saved my foot.

---

both worked hard and had so many good times and laughs together. It seemed that someone would always come in at the last minute after we had straightened all the socks and they would want the pair on the bottom and turn the bin of socks up-side-down. I could actually write a whole book on all the things that transpired during those two years. It was fun, interesting and memories I will treasure forever. We still reminisce even after all these years. You see, Mary Lou married my oldest brother and they will celebrate their 60th wedding anniversary in December 2012.

In my junior year I won a trip to Winthrop College for a weekend to see if that was the college I wanted to attend. In my junior year I also did something that taught me a valuable lesson. I failed U. S. History and I had to take it over my senior year. The sad part was what the teacher told me. I had realized, too late, that I wasn't going to pass History and I went to the teacher and I begged her to let me do a report or something to earn the 2 points I needed to pass the course. It is strange how you remember the teachers that made an impression on you, usually because you needed to learn a specific lesson. She told me that I was too smart to be let go so easily. I needed to realize that an education was the most important gift we could give ourselves and it would benefit us for the rest of our lives and especially important was U. S. History. At that time I could only see that I would have to give up my free period my senior year to retake U. S. History. She also said that if I had paid a little more attention to the lessons presented rather than the boys in the class, that I would have had no problem passing the class. Well, needless to say, I took U. S. History in my free period my senior year and I passed it with an A. I didn't learn to like history, but I did learn that if you have to do something, then do your best or be willing to pay the consequences.

During my senior year I also received my driver's license. As with everything else in my life there is an interesting story about it. Daddy had taken me on the route that I would be asked to drive in order to obtain my license several times so I knew it really well. I passed the written test and was waiting for the policeman to take me on the driving portion when daddy whispered to me to not get flustered and remember the route. The policeman motioned for me to go to the car. I was so conscious of the route that I wasn't listening to the policeman. I followed the path

Perfectly and when we arrived back at the station I was sure that I had passed. The policeman said he was sorry but I would not receive my license that day. I asked why? He told me that I did not listen to him. He told me that after the first turn he felt I had earned my license so he told me to turn left and go back to the station. He said that I totally ignored him and turned right and continued to complete the route without listening to anything he said. He told me that he felt I did not know the difference between left and right and that could be very detrimental on the highway.

He then broke my heart when he said, "You need to go home and learn your right from your left. You can come back next week and try again." At that time you could only try for your license once

The third miracle. An accident and God saved my foot.

a week. I was angry and very disappointed, but I went back the next week expecting to do the whole test over.

When I walked in to the station, the policeman looked at me and said, "Hold up your left hand." I raised my left hand and he said, "Do you want paper or metal?" I said "metal". That was all it took. I have to confess that after all these years I still have difficulty realizing right from left. Jerry told me to remember that my wedding rings were on my left hand. That helped sometimes.

I have one more confession to make. This situation happened when I was in the 12th grade and I was 16 years old. I was very self-centered and as I said had a very high self-esteem and I was dating a young man who attended my church and we went to school together. His name was Beverly and he wanted to be called Beverly because he wanted to be different. He had studied piano most of his life and was an excellent pianist. His life's goal was to become a concert pianist. Every time he came over we would spend hours playing the piano and singing. In fact, that's all he ever wanted to do. He was not interested in going to a movie or anything except music. Now, I love music, but I also wanted to do other things, like movies, go to the park, etc. While I was dating him I was also a cheerleader and this led to my disobeying my mother one night. We had play practice at church. I had planned to go to play practice and then to the football game. For some reason, mother said I could go to play practice, but not to the game. The game started unusually late for some reason and it was on a school night. After play practice, I went to the game with the others, cheered, and had a wonderful time, except for my nagging conscience that knew mother had said I couldn't go to the game.

It was after 11 when Beverly dropped me off. Mother was very upset with me and restricted me for two weeks. I could only go to school, work, church, and ball games. No friends over and no talking on the phone. Plus, Beverly couldn't come over and I couldn't talk to him. During that time, Beverly decided he wanted to concentrate on his music and not me.

As I said, I was spoiled and very self-centered so I decided to make Beverly jealous. I flirted with a guy who worked at the local grocery store. His name was Robert. He was older – 22 years old. I had to walk past the grocery store on my way to and from school. We actually never dated. We would talk on my way home from school. After a few weeks, on my way home one day Robert said that he was in love with me and wanted to marry me. He had an engagement ring, which I accepted even though I knew I didn't love him, and of course my mother was very upset with me and told me to return the ring. I told her I would as soon as I flashed it around to see if this would make Beverly jealous. She really gave me a lecture about playing with people's feelings, but I didn't listen. Consequently, this didn't work out like I had hoped it would. It didn't make Beverly jealous and I was stuck with an engagement ring from someone I didn't like, much less love, but who loved me.

Since I wasn't having any luck with Beverly, I knew I would have to return the ring to Robert and tell him I didn't love him. It never occurred to me how much I would hurt him. I was only thinking of myself. I gave Robert the ring back and told him my parents felt he was too old for me and I had a scholarship for college and would not be getting married anytime soon. I felt really bad – for a little while – as I said, I'm not proud of leading him on for selfish purposes.

High school days were exciting and I loved being involved in everything from cheerleading to drama presentations, and singing in the glee club and beautifying the school grounds. Oh, yes, classes were fun and interesting, but not very challenging except for U. S. History.

Besides school activities, church, and work, I also had a life changing experience. I attended Rutledge Ave. Baptist Church and Anna Mims was the director of music and she was also my voice and piano teacher. I was trained to sing opera and every time I had a recital my father would ask, "Is this what I am paying for?" The only music he really enjoyed was church music or country music.

When I was thirteen, Ms. Mims was also my Sunday School teacher and one Sunday she talked about how to become a Christian and making Jesus the Lord of our lives and I realized that although I had been baptized when I was 10 I had never really had a personal experience with Jesus and asked Him to forgive me and come into my life and lead me through this life and take me to heaven when I died. Like so many people who grow up attending church, it seemed as though God and Jesus had always been a vital part of my life. However, on that day, Ms. Mims made it very clear that we were saved by grace, not by works; it was a gift, freely given by Jesus when he died on the cross for everyone's sins which included my sins. She said that through his resurrection Jesus conquered death and sin. She said that the wages of sin was death and that anyone who believed Jesus was the son of God and asked forgiveness from individual sins and invited Jesus to come and live in their heart would be saved and have the promise of eternal life in heaven with God, the Father, Jesus the Son and the Holy Spirit.

So when the invitation was given in church that Sunday morning I asked God to forgive me of my sins and to come into my heart. I wanted to live for Him. Church and everything I did after that seemed to be more meaningful and I knew I had a purpose to fulfill. Shortly after that Ms. Mims asked me to teach the 4 and 5 year olds in choir. The choir was called the Cherub Choir and sang in the worship service once each month. I accepted. It didn't take long for me to realize that music was going to be an important part of my life. So, at thirteen, I started directing the Cherub Choir and did so until after I graduated from high school. All too soon, those years flew by and then I was sixteen and graduating from high school and preparing to go to college.

Jr., Nellie, Gene,
LeRoy, Janie, Faye

Both of my brothers had joined the Air Force. They took leave and came home for my graduation. That night my brothers, their

The third miracle. An accident and God saved my foot.

dates and mine went out. I had never been to a club. In fact there had never been any alcohol in my home and we were not even allowed to play Old Maid cards. My parents implanted strong Christian values and standards in us as we grew up. After my brothers joined the service, some of their activities had changed. We went to Andre's, a popular club near Folly Beach. When the waitress took our order for drinks I listened while others ordered mixed drinks. I didn't know what they were so when my date, Sonny, asked me what I wanted to drink I replied, "I'll have a Tom Collins." Now I didn't know Tom from Joe, but I had heard someone order that so I thought it would be alright for me to order one.

Senior Prom

Both my brothers stood up and said in a loud voice, "You will not! You will have a coke and nothing in it!" I was humiliated. I had graduated earlier that day. I felt I was grown up and could order a drink if I wanted one. Poor innocent me. I didn't realize what drinking would do or could do to a person. I had a coke and to this day, many years later, I have never had a drink. I don't know one kind of drink from the other and I really don't feel that I have missed anything. I thank my brothers for looking out for me.

Chapter Five:

The fourth miracle- Meeting the Love of my Life

"For this cause shall a man leave his father and mother, and shall be joined unto his wife, and they two shall be one flesh."

Ephesians 5:31

My father worked for the Newspaper in Charleston and they had offered me a full scholarship if I would major in journalism and after graduating I would come and work for them for 4 years as a reporter. That sounded exciting so I accepted the scholarship and was planning on attending the University of South Carolina in Columbia, South Carolina in August, 1952. I continued to work for Mr. Ed, but in a different capacity. Knowing I was going to college in the fall, Mr. Ed offered me the opportunity to work in the office (at that time Mr. Ed had opened 9 stores throughout South Carolina) as receptionist and assistant hosiery buyer for the 9 stores until I left to go to college. Of course I accepted it and it was exciting and challenging. The salesmen always brought gifts to encourage me to "get them in to see the buyers" and I had the chance to sit in and listen

The fourth miracle - Meeting the Love of my Life

to the conversations between the salesmen and the buyers. This was a great learning experience for me. At the same time I was dating a young man, Henry, – actually several young men – but this one was special, but he lived in Charlotte, North Carolina and was a friend of my cousin, Billy, who lived in Charlotte. He was already in college in Georgia. My cousin lived in Charlotte and I had met Henry when I had visited Billy and his wife. Henry and I had been writing each other and the July 4th holiday was approaching. He wrote and asked me to visit my cousin over the holiday weekend so we could go out. My parents agreed and I asked Mary Lou to go with me to Charlotte for the July 4th weekend. It was arranged and I was excited. At that time I was 5' 3" tall and weighed 98 pounds. My daddy picked Mary Lou and me up at 5 p.m. from work and took us straight to the bus station. He said we had a layover in Columbia, but he didn't know how long.

When we arrived in Columbia, all we saw in the bus station were tan uniforms – soldiers – and we were fascinated because coming from Charleston all we were used to seeing were Citadel cadets and sailors. We were standing in the bus station trying to decide what to do. You must understand at this point that both of us had been raised in strict Christian homes and had never been anywhere without our parents so this was a situation with lots of mixed emotions. We wanted to be brave and try something new, but we were alone and also very afraid because we didn't have parents with us to help us know what to do.

Twelve Miracles Including a Glimpse of Heaven

As we were standing near one of the lines to purchase tickets a gentleman came up to us and said to the soldiers standing in line, "Why don't one of you good looking soldiers let these young ladies in line."

At that time, one of the soldiers did a little bow and offered us a place in line. I looked at the handsome soldier and all I could see was big, beautiful, brown eyes that seemed to see right through me.

I quickly spoke up and said, "We don't need to buy tickets, we just need to know what time the bus leaves for Charlotte."

The young man said, "That's where I'm going. I'll let you know."

When the soldier in front of the young man bought his ticket he came over to us and said, "If you girls have some time to kill, let's go dancing."

When he said that, the trigger in my brain clicked in and my strict Christian upbringing kicked in and probably a little fear of the unknown and I said, "No thank you. We don't know you and we're not from here so we will wait right here in the bus station."

About that time the handsome, young man with the big, beautiful, brown eyes walked up and said that the bus didn't leave until 9:30 and he told me later that I looked so skinny he was afraid I was hungry so his next words to us were, "Would you'll like to go get something to eat?"

I looked at this young man standing next to me and all I could see was big, beautiful, brown eyes that seemed to see through me, but again my conscience kicked in and I said, "I'm sorry, but we don't know you either and we're not leaving the bus station."

The fourth miracle- Meeting the Love of my Life

Very calmly he said, "Let's look at this logically. This is a public place and we are one block from Main Street and it is well lighted and there are four of us to provide protection for each other. We'll just walk down Main Street to a restaurant which will be well lighted and public and get something to eat and then come back in time to catch the bus for Charlotte."

I looked at Mary Lou and she looked at me and we knew we hadn't taken time to eat and we were hungry and what he said made sense so we agreed to go to the restaurant. He was right when he said it was Main Street and everything was lit up. We walked about 4 blocks towards the State House and across from the State House was a restaurant. We went in and for some reason I wasn't hungry anymore. I only ordered a coke. I really don't remember what the others ordered. As we sat at the table we found out a little more about each other. He said he had been in the Army for almost two years. He said he was in supply school at Fort Jackson and would be finished in about a month and then he would go back to his unit in Fayetteville, NC. I

Nellie

had some of my graduation pictures in my purse and I pulled one out and wrote on the back of the picture, Remember me, the Charlestonian and I wrote my address on it and gave it to him. He told me his name was Jerry Hartsoe, but honestly all I could remember was Jerry and those big, beautiful, brown eyes. He was 6 feet tall and very handsome. He said he was going to visit his cousin in Kannapolis and would it be alright if he sat with me on the bus to Charlotte. Mary Lou agreed to sit across the aisle and so on the bus that night Jerry and I sat right behind the bus driver and Mary Lou sat across the aisle.

It was almost 2 hours to Charlotte so we talked a lot. He said he didn't have any brothers or sisters and had lived with his grandmother until he was 13 and she died. He then went to live in Pennsylvania with his mother and step-father. He said his mother and step-father owned a dairy farm and he had worked on it while going to high school. During the summer before his senior year he joined the Army Reserves and his unit was activated because of the Korean conflict. By the time they realized his age and discharged him he had missed the first half of his senior year. He was told that he couldn't graduate with his class so he talked his mother into signing for him to go back on active duty with the Army. He was beginning his 3rd year of a four year enlistment. He said his step-father had died in May of that year and his mother moved back to North Carolina. He said he didn't have a steady girl friend and was it possible that he could see me while I was visiting in Charlotte. I knew I already had plans to date Henry so I said no, I already had plans. He asked if he could ride back on the bus with me Sunday afternoon as far as Columbia. I said I guessed that would be o.k.

The fourth miracle- Meeting the Love of my Life

I was excited all weekend and all I could talk about was Jerry some-thing-another (I couldn't remember or pronounce his last name) and his big brown eyes and that I hoped I would see him again. Of course that didn't make Henry happy. We had a wonderful weekend, swimming and picnicking, but all too soon it was time to go back to Charleston. I was actually looking forward to the bus ride home, but we were late getting to the bus station and Mary and I got on a bus marked Charleston. I didn't see Jerry on the bus, but there were a lot of sailor's going back to Charleston and they overheard me say I was looking for Jerry and so they started calling out the window to people standing by the buses. They kept saying, "Hey, Jerry, where are you?" Then I saw him. He was standing by the bus window looking in all directions. He heard the guys yelling his name and he came over to the bus. I didn't recognize him at first because when I met him he was wearing his uniform and now he had on civilian clothes. I still remember seeing him in a long-sleeve light blue shirt, white undershirt and tan slacks. He looked even more handsome and his brown eyes were sparkling and he said the bus we had gotten on didn't go through Columbia so he couldn't get on it. He asked if he could come to Charleston to see me and I said I had strict parents and he would have to write me and I would ask my parents and write him back. He had my address, but I didn't have his.

When I went out my mother would go to bed, but she never went to sleep until I was safely in the house. I always had a habit of going into her bedroom and sitting on the side of the bed and telling her everything we did. I told her what was said, where we went, and just talked and talked. She always listened and then she would say,

"O. K., I'm glad you had a good time, now go to bed, because I'm going to sleep now that you are safely home."

Of course, as usual, I told my parents about Jerry (I still couldn't pronounce his last name). I asked if it would be alright for him to come to visit me. My mother said that he could come, but he would have to stay in a hotel, go to church with us on Sunday and leave my house on Saturday night by 11 which was my time to be home. I got a letter from Jerry on Tuesday and I answered it and told him what Mother had said. I didn't get a letter back but on Saturday, I was sitting on the front porch and Jerry came walking down the street. I was so excited, my heart started beating really fast. He was a private first class and didn't make much money. He didn't have a car and only had enough money for the hotel room so he said he had hitchhiked from Columbia to Charleston and had gotten a ride to the corner from my house. We talked and talked all afternoon and evening.

Jerry told me that he needed to tell me something that might make a difference in how I felt about him. Needless to say I was curious. He continued to tell me that when his mother was 17 she got pregnant and he didn't have a father. He lived with his grandparents until he was 13 and his grandmother died. They lived in Jefferson, North Carolina and after his grandmother died he went to live with his mother and step-father. His mother had married when Jerry was about 10 years old, but he had continued to live with his grandmother. He wanted to know if it made a difference to me that he was born before his mother was married and that she had never married his father. I told him that it didn't make a difference to me. He didn't ask to be born and he was not responsible for the choices his parents had made. He told me he was glad because he felt I was going to be someone special in his life and how he was born was important to him and he just wanted to know if it would change my mind about him. He also asked me to go steady with him and I said, no. He wanted to know why and I told him it was because he didn't live in Charleston and was not always here and I liked to go out and if I went out with someone else it wouldn't be fair to him. I told him if he would let me know when he could come to Charleston I would always make time to spend with him. He said he only had a couple more weeks of school and would be returning to Fayetteville, NC soon and since that was further away he didn't know how often he would get to come.

That first weekend with Jerry (I still couldn't pronounce his last name) was almost magical and yet, all we did was talk and talk until he had to leave to go find a hotel. He was back the next morning in time to go to church with us. Mother usually cooked lunch early on Sunday morning and we would go to Sunday School and church and then head to the beach to eat a picnic lunch, swim and enjoy the beach until late afternoon and then get home in time to get cleaned up so we could go back to Training Union and Church on Sunday evenings.

It is also strange that none of my boyfriends met my father's approval except Jerry. In fact, the first time he came, daddy told me to take the car (my father didn't lend his car – he always said that there were two things you didn't lend and that was your car and your wife – in that order) and take Jerry out to the north area so he could catch a ride easier.

That next week all I could talk about was Jerry. I can't say that I was in love with him, but I knew he was different. I couldn't wait until the next time I saw him. One of the young men I was dating at that time was named Tommy and he seemed to know something was different about me and he wanted to know all about Jerry. I told him it wasn't anything for him to worry about because Jerry wasn't in town and I probably wouldn't ever see him again. Tommy and I made a date for the following Saturday night. Little did I know that by Saturday night I would be in double trouble?

I was getting ready for my date on that Saturday when the phone rang. My little sister (who always seemed to be in the living room when I had a date) answered the phone. She called me and said Jerry is on the phone. I ran downstairs and answered the phone. I asked him where he was and he said he was where he could see me in five minutes if it was alright. Of course I said it was and to come on over. He was at the store on the corner. I panicked and went in to the kitchen and told mother that Jerry was on his way and would be there in a few minutes and I was supposed to go out with Tommy and I needed her to tell Tommy when he got there that something came up and I couldn't go out.

The fourth miracle - Meeting the Love of my Life

She just looked at me and said, "No, you got yourself in double trouble, you have to get yourself out of it." Again she reminded me about using people and that it was selfish because after Jerry left I would still want Tommy and Johnny (Johnny was another really cute, nice guy I was dating, but mother didn't approve of him because she said she didn't like the way his pants fit – that he didn't have a behind). It didn't matter to me, but mother always wanted people to be dressed nicely and their clothes to fit. She always commented on my friends according to how they dressed. That was important to her, not so much to me.

True to his word, Jerry was at the door in five minutes and I invited him in. Time he came in he said, "You've got a date, haven't you?"

I said, "Yes, but I'm not going to go. I'll tell him you came in town unexpectedly and it wouldn't be polite of me not to spend time with you since you came a long way and I can see him later because he lives here."

Jerry said it would be o.k. for me to go since he didn't let me know he was coming. About that time, Tommy rang the doorbell. I went to the door and told him that something had come up and I wouldn't be able to go out.

He saw Jerry in the living room and said, "Is that the something that came up?"

I said, "Yes, I didn't know he was coming in town and it wouldn't be right for me to go off and leave him."

Tommy said, "I think I ought to meet him since he is my competition."

I said, "No, I don't think that's a good idea."

Tommy called out to my mother and said, "Hey, Mom, don't you think I should meet my

competition?" (All my friends called my mother, Mom.)

My mother came out of the kitchen and said, "Sure, Tommy, come on in." (I gave my mother a look that would kill.) Tommy came into the living room. I introduced them and we all sat down. I sat on the piano bench; Jerry sat in the chair; and Tommy sat on the couch.

My sister, Faye, came in and said, "If you'll give me a quarter, I'll leave." (She had a habit of getting my dates to give her a quarter to leave us alone.) Tommy told her to sit by him. She did and for over an hour, we tried to make conversation. It was a disaster.

Finally, Tommy said, "Well, I guess I better go. Walk me to the door."

I said o.k. and excused myself and walked Tommy to the door.

This next part is a subject that my husband and I disagreed on throughout our marriage and our children thoroughly enjoyed listening to our discussions about it.

As Tommy was about to leave he leaned forward to kiss me and I put my hand up and said, "No, not now."

He said, "Why, because of him? Well, he may have cheated me out of my date tonight, but he's not going to cheat me out of my goodnight kiss."

The fourth miracle- Meeting the Love of my Life

I said, "He's not going to cheat you out of anything because you didn't have one to begin with. He'll leave Sunday afternoon, come over around 6 and we'll go to church and get something to drink afterward to make up for tonight." He said o.k. and left.

For 52 years Jerry still believed that I kissed Tommy goodnight and for 52 years I know that I was right and I did not kiss Tommy goodnight. Our children enjoyed hearing the story since Jerry had one opinion and I had the true opinion. For some reason they tended to believe their father's version rather than mine. Only God and I know the truth. I didn't kiss Tommy.

I went back into the living room and Jerry said, "Let's go out on the porch."

I said o.k. and we went out on the porch and sat in the porch swing. He said he appreciated my cancelling my date. I told him that anytime he was in town I would always give him first choice. He, again, asked me to go steady. I explained to him why I wouldn't go steady with him. It would be unfair to him and to me. He said he wouldn't make any more visits without first letting me know he was coming. He said he was finishing his school and would be transferred back to Fayetteville in two weeks.

During the next two weeks, we wrote to each other. I knew that my family's reunion was coming up the next weekend. It had been three weeks since I had seen Jerry. My grandparents lived in the country near Pamplico, SC and my parents said it was o.k to invite Jerry to the reunion and that he could come to Florence and someone would pick him up and he could spend the night at my aunt's home. I was excited thinking about seeing him. I knew there was something special about him but I didn't know if it was love.

Finally, the weekend of the reunion came and my brother picked Jerry up at the bus station in Florence and brought him to my aunt's house. My brother (oldest) and my girlfriend (Mary Lou) were planning on announcing their engagement that weekend and we were all looking forward to a December wedding for them. It was wonderful to see Jerry. He looked so handsome in his uniform. He was in a soldier's uniform and my brother was in his Air Force uniform. They both looked great in their uniforms – as my mother said, their uniforms really fit.

The reunion was on Sunday after church. Everyone in the family came – my father was one of six and they were all there and their children and my grandparents. There was so much food. I really miss those times. After we ate, my grandfather always gathered us around him as he sat in the big swing on the porch and he would tell us stories, some of them were true and some he made up. After he had a stroke and couldn't talk very much, my father became the story teller and we loved listening to the stories and his singing.

It was almost time for Jerry to leave to catch the bus back to Fayetteville. We were walking down the dirt road and he, again, asked me to go steady with him. I, again, told him no, but this time I added something.

I said, "I won't go steady with you, but I'll marry you if you want me to."

The fourth miracle - Meeting the Love of my Life

He said, "Yes, I do."

I said, "O.k. when do you want to get married?"

He said, "I used my leave time when my step-father died, but I have a long weekend in three weeks. It will be Labor Day and I have off Saturday through Monday. I don't have to be back until Tuesday morning."

I said, "O.K. Let's go tell the family." I WAS JOKING. We went in the house and said, "Everybody listen, we're getting married Labor Day weekend."

Everybody said, "Yeah, sure, o.k." They all thought we were joking.

Then it was time for my brother to take Jerry back to Florence to catch the bus back to Fayetteville.

When he left he said, "See you in three weeks."

I said, "O.K."

He said, "I love you."

I said, "I love you, too." That was the first time either one had said the love word.

The day I proposed to Jerry

The next week I received a letter from Jerry. He asked if it would be o.k. for him to bring his mother with him for our wedding.

I read the letter to mother and she said, "It sounds like he is serious and you better make up your mind if you are serious."

I said, I was joking, but he is really cute and I do like him better than anyone else.

She asked, "Do you have to get married?"

I said, "No, but it might be fun."

She said, "What about college?"

I told her I would still go to college.

Then she said, "Well, if you're serious, why don't you have a double wedding with Jr. and Mary Lou in December."

I said, "No, if I'm going to get married, I don't want a church wedding. I want to get married here at home. I want to walk down the stairs, through the French doors and get married in front of the fireplace." I was thinking of "Gone with the Wind" and I thought it would be romantic to glide down the stairs and through the French doors. I didn't want a wedding dress. I wanted to get married in blue (my favorite color).

I wrote Jerry and told him it would be fine to bring his mother. I told him since he couldn't get to Charleston until Saturday, my cousin Betty and her husband would pretend to be us and go to Summerville to put in for our license. So, that is what Betty and Leonard did. They pretended to be Jerry and me and put in for our license, but we had to pick the license up on Saturday. Mother and I went shopping for a blue dress. As it turns out, I found a light blue two piece suit. I was so small (18" waist, 5' 3", 100 pounds) that mother had to take it up to make it fit like she wanted it to fit. We ordered the cake and invited a few friends. The wedding was to take place on Sunday, August 31 at 4:00 p.m.

The fourth miracle- Meeting the Love of my Life

Jerry and his mother arrived about 11 a.m. on Saturday, August 30, 1952. His mother smoked and had dropped ashes on her dress and wanted to buy something new so he had taken her downtown and dropped her off and then came to pick me up. He didn't remember where he had dropped her off and so we rode up and down Main Street and I didn't even know what she looked like. Finally, he saw her and stopped to pick her up. She was tall, slender, had brown eyes and brown hair. When she got in the car I scooted over next to Jerry and she sat next to me.

Her first words were, "I don't know why you dropped me off in this part of town. There were no stores with clothes."

I said, "I'm sorry, he doesn't know where the dress shops are since he hasn't been down town before."

She said, "Well, I guess it is o.k." We sat quietly on the ride home. We dropped her off and left her with my mother. We went to Summerville to pick up our license. When we got to the justice of the peace's house Jerry only had a twenty dollar bill and the license was three dollars. The justice of the peace didn't have any change so I pulled out three one dollar bills and paid for the license. We left and Jerry stopped at the first service station he came to. He went inside and came back out and handed me three one dollar bills.

I said, "What is this for?"

He said, "I don't want you telling everyone you had to pay for our license." When we got back home, sitting in the car (which was his mothers) he pulled out a ring box and opened it to show a beautiful set of wedding rings. He took the engagement ring out of the box and took my hand and put the ring on my finger and looked at me with those big brown eyes and said, "Now, it's official. You will marry me, won't you?"

I said, "Yes, I will since I don't have anything better to do." He reached over and hugged me. He also asked me if I had had anything to do with anyone else. He quickly added that it wouldn't make any difference, but since he was going to be my husband he felt he had a right to know. Frankly, I really didn't understand what he was talking about, but it felt like he was insulting me.

I quickly responded and took the ring off my finger and said, "No, I haven't had anything to do with anyone else, but if that's the kind of girl you think I am, then you can have this ring back."

He quickly put the ring back on my finger and said, "Well, thank goodness that's over with."

I said, "What's over with?" He said, "Our first argument. I believe you." I was a little confused because I still didn't really know what he was talking about. I just knew it didn't sound right.

The next day was Sunday and we went to church, as usual, and then to the beach and back home to get ready to get married. My pastor was out of town so we had asked Mary Lou's principal who was an ordained minister to perform the ceremony. He wanted to talk to Jerry and me before he married us. We sat in the living room while mother and my aunt prepared the refreshments for after the ceremony.

Rev. Corder said, "Marriage is a serious step for you young people to take. I have three guidelines concerning your lives and your marriage to share with you and if you will commit yourselves to accept these guidelines and follow them you will have a wonderful, long marriage.

The first guideline is to make Jesus the Lord of your lives and the cornerstone of your marriage. Be sure to include Him in every decision you make and ask Him to guide your daily walk with Him. The second guideline is to keep the lines of communication open. No matter how small or large something is, talk to each other, honestly and openly about it. Little things left to simmer will grow and become mountains that will be difficult to climb, but if you talk about it and agree to agree, or agree to disagree and still love each other, there won't be any mountain or valley you can't get through together. The third guideline is perhaps the hardest of all to keep. The third guideline is, never go to bed mad. Always settle your differences before you go to sleep because you never know if there will be a tomorrow to talk about it."

I can say that Jerry and I kept the first two guidelines without any problem (almost), but the third one took a lot of work. Sometimes we didn't get much sleep, but we would finally settle whatever the problem was and agree to agree or agree to disagree but acknowledge that we still loved each other even though we might not agree on everything. Those three guidelines provided us with a marriage that lasted almost 52 years, until Jerry's death parted us temporarily. The reason this chapter is called the fourth miracle is because I believe it was a miracle and predestined that Jerry and I would meet, fall in love and get married. At 16 (I was 17 18 days later) and 18 (Jerry was 19 4 days later) I don't believe either of us really understood what love and marriage really meant. God knew and He knew we belonged together so I believe He arranged our meeting in that bus station and walked every step with us throughout the 51 ½ years He gave us. One day I will join my precious husband and we will never be separated again.

At 4 p.m. on Sunday, August 31, 1952 my father walked me down the stairs and through the French doors and presented me to Jerry. I had on my light blue two-piece suit with a corsage of yellow roses. Jerry wore his uniform. He always looked so handsome in his uniform. Mary Lou was my maid of honor and my cousin Clayton was visiting and he became Jerry's best man. After our vows were said and rings exchanged, Rev. Corder pronounced us husband and wife and Jerry kissed me. We had met the Fourth of July weekend; saw each other on three weekends and on August 31st we became husband and wife. We had never gone out on a real "date". It

Wedding Day
August 31, 1952

all seemed like a dream. We cut our cake and shared refreshments with our guests. At 5:30 p.m. we went to church and attended

The fourth miracle- Meeting the Love of my Life

Training Union (I had a part on program so I had to be there) and church. At that time everything closed on Sunday by five o'clock and we had not had supper so we tried to find something open to get something to eat, but there were no restaurants open so we stopped at a gas station and bought some peanut butter-cheese crackers and

Cutting our Wedding Cake

cokes. That became our wedding night supper. We drove across the Cooper River Bridge and stopped at a new motel just across the bridge. The motel had a sitting room and a separate bedroom with two double beds and a bath. There was a coin music box in the sitting room. Jerry put a quarter in the music box and picked an Elvis song (I don't remember the name of it) and as the song began to play we opened the crackers and cokes and began eating. He was sitting in a chair and I was on the sofa.

He said, "Remember what I asked you yesterday?"

I said, "What, you asked me a lot of things."

He said, "The thing about you having had something to do with someone else."

I still didn't know what he was talking about, but I said, "Yes, what about it?"

He said, "Well, I believe you now."

I said, "What do you mean, you believe me now."

He said, "You couldn't be this scared if you had had something to do with someone else."

I said, "I really don't know what you are talking about, but I'm glad you believe me."

Later, I went into the bathroom to change into my gown and get ready for bed. I locked the door. I took out my gown (it was light green, floor length, trimmed with lace). I put my hands in the bottom of the gown and began to slip it over my head and all of a sudden I realized that I couldn't get my hands and arms to go in the right place in the gown. I took it off and saw that the arm holds had been sown together with the same color thread so it could not be seen. I screamed and Jerry ran to the door and tried to come into the bathroom, but couldn't because it was locked.

He asked, "What is wrong?"

I replied, "Aunt Myrtle (somehow I knew it was her since she had offered to pack my overnight bag) sewed up my gown."

He said, "Well, open the door and I'll help you rip it out."

I said, "No thank you." I put my clothes back on and fully dressed I walked out of the bathroom and said, "I'll take this bed and you can have that one." Then, fully dressed, I went to bed and to sleep. Jerry lay down on the other bed and that's how we spent our wedding night.

The next morning we went to a restaurant for breakfast and then to my house. Mother and Jerry's mother had prepared a picnic and everyone went to the beach since it was Labor Day.

The fourth miracle- Meeting the Love of my Life

We swam, ate, played and had a wonderful time at the beach, but all too soon, the time came for Jerry to leave to go back to Fayetteville, NC. He was going to drop his mother off at his aunt's house in Jefferson, NC and she was going to let him keep the car so he could come back to Charleston the next weekend.

Jerry commuted back and forth for the next month. Of course, I lost my scholarship and so I went back to work in the office at Edward's. After a month I decided I didn't like being a weekend wife so I went to Fayetteville and we found an apartment and I moved there the first of October. I had never learned to cook. I could make cookies. I learned how to do that while taking Home Economics in high school. The first meal I cooked was horrible. I tried to fry chicken and burned it. I cooked rice and it was sticky and gummy. I opened a can of peas and I couldn't get them to taste like the ones mother made. I kept putting salt and cooking oil in them, but they just wouldn't taste like mothers. (Later I found that I had bought sugar peas and mother always bought garden peas. Nothing can make sugar peas taste like garden peas.) I also made biscuits. Jerry was so sweet. He ate the burned chicken, put the sugar peas over the rice and tried to swallow it. He almost broke a tooth on the biscuits because they were like little bricks. I cried and he hugged me and told me it was the best meal he had ever eaten. (Sometime later he asked if I had saved the recipe I used to make the biscuits. I asked why, and he said he thought he would send it to the Pentagon because they could use it to make bombs). I cried some more and he hugged me some more and said he was kidding.

I needed to work because our total income was $157 month. Rent was $60 a month and so I got a job at Department store in Fayetteville. That was not a good move because I was a soldier's wife and subject to leave town if my husband was transferred, so I was hired to stock the shelves. I felt humiliated because I had so much experience and I was being penalized for being married to a soldier. After 3 weeks, I was very angry.

I had had a very bad day and Jerry came home and jokingly said, "O. K. wife, get the supper on the table, I'm hungry."

That was the straw that broke the camels back so to speak and I said, "If you want your supper on the table you can put it there. I am sick of being a soldier's wife, I don't want to be a soldier's wife, and I just kept repeating it over and over."

Jerry said in a calm voice, "shut up, Nellie, and you don't need to go back to work, you just quit."

I didn't calm down or shut up and I was almost hysterical I was so angry and upset.

Once again, in a calm voice, Jerry said, "shut up Nellie, you don't mean what you are saying."

I screamed at him saying that I did mean it. He reached over and slapped me gently on the cheek. I was so startled I just stared at him. It did shut me up. I walked out of the apartment and went and sat on the front porch of the house and cried. I thought Jerry would come after me and hug me, apologize for hitting me, and wipe away my

The fourth miracle - Meeting the Love of my Life

tears and my pain. Wrong! He didn't come after me and after about an hour of pouting, I went back to the apartment.

He asked me if I felt better.

I said, "No."

He said, "You don't have to go back to work there. We will make out somehow. After all, you always say that the Lord will provide."

I guess I need to tell you that God and church and my Christian life had been so very important to me since I had accepted Jesus as my Savior at the age of 13. I knew that Jerry was not a Christian, and on the weekend we decided to get married I had told him that Jesus was first in my life and that if we married he would never complain about my serving the Lord no matter how much time it took. He had agreed that he didn't have a problem with my relationship to Jesus. My favorite saying was, "The Lord will provide." I guess I wasn't very mature in my Christian walk at that time because I just simply trusted that when you loved the Lord and served Him that He would take care of everything. Remember, I had just turned 17 (Sept. 18) and had always lived with mother and daddy who took care of everything.

The next day I turned in my resignation and went home concerned that we needed the money, but I didn't want to stock shelves. I thought about the scholarship I had given up and somehow wished I had opted for going on to school. When Jerry came in that afternoon, he had a big family Bible with him. It was beautiful, but I knew it was expensive. I asked him how he had paid for it.

He calmly, with assurance, said, "I know how important the Bible is to you and you said you wanted a family Bible and this man was at the base today selling them and he said the same thing you always say, 'The Lord will provide' and so I bought it for you to make you feel better."

I said, "I Love it, but how much did it cost and where did you get the money to pay for it?"

He said, "It cost $40 and I used part of the rent money to pay for it."

I said, "How are we going to pay rent in 4 days?"

He just looked at me and said, "The Lord will provide."

Two days later, two days before rent was due, Jerry came in and said, "You know, you and that man that sold me the Bible were right. The Lord really does provide."

I said, "What do you mean?"

He said, "Well, we don't have to pay rent for next month. I just got orders to go to Korea so you will have to go home and you can go to school because I will be gone 13 months."

I was floored, but that's what happened. Within a week my husband, whom I had known all of 4 months was on his way to Korea and I was on my way home and school.

The fourth miracle - Meeting the Love of my Life

Jerry in Korea 1952

It was a very long 13 months, but Jerry wrote every day he was away. I can't say that I was that faithful, but I did try to write a couple times a week. Then on November 14, 1953 Jerry called and said he was at Fort Jackson, SC and wanted me to come to Columbia.

While he was in Korea, I bought the first car we ever owned. It

first car 1946 Chev.

was a 1946 Chevrolet and I paid $600 for it. I drove to Columbia with mother, daddy and Faye following me in their car. I had our wedding picture with me because I wasn't sure I would remember how he looked and the picture

Wedding Picture

would help. While sitting in the car on Fort Jackson, I kept looking at all the soldier's and wondering if each one was him. Finally, I saw those big brown eyes, looking so handsome in his uniform heading straight for the car. I was so excited to see him. We all went to a restaurant and ate supper and then mother, daddy and Faye went back to Columbia. Jerry's enlistment was over and he would be discharged in a few days so we stayed in a motel on Jackson Blvd. so he would be close to the base until he received his discharge papers. We went home to Charleston.

Jerry had decided to go to school in Kansas City, MO. He wanted to study electronics and I could transfer and go to school in Kansas City. Of course that meant I would lose my scholarship, again. We left in November 1953 for Kansas City. It was exciting. I knew I would have to work and go to school because the money he would get to go to school wouldn't be enough. I got a job in a bank and we rented an apartment and we registered for school to begin in January. Things were going well for us and then I found that I was pregnant and in December 1953 I had a miscarriage and all I wanted to do was go home. I wanted my mother. Jerry said that he could still go back in service at his same rank since it had not been 90 days since he was discharged so we packed up our belongings and headed back to Charleston.

Christmas was a time to put everything aside and realize that God had a plan for us. In January, 1954 Jerry re-enlisted in the Army and retained his rank of Sgt. He asked to be assigned to the base in Boston, MA. He had been there a short while during his first enlistment and wanted to show me how beautiful the country was there. Since we didn't have housing in Boston, I stayed with his aunt and uncle that we called Mammaw and Papaw in Cockranville, PA which was only a few hours away from where he was stationed. His aunt and uncle owned a chicken farm and it was so pleasant staying there.

The fourth miracle- Meeting the Love of my Life

During the week I helped with the canning and feeding the chickens and Jerry would come on the weekends.

In March, 1954, Jerry passed the test for Officer's Candidate School (OCS) and on April 9, we packed all our belongings (which included my cedar chest that Mother and Daddy had given me for graduation) in our new car (we had traded the 1946 Chevrolet for a 1954 Chevrolet – in fact, we had only made one payment on it) and headed to Charleston so we could spend the weekend with my family before heading to Fort Gordon, GA where Jerry would be in OCS school.

Chapter Six:

The fifth miracle - Out of Body experience

"Rejoice in the Lord alway: and again I say, Rejoice. Let your moderation be known unto all men. The Lord is at hand. Be careful for nothing; but in everything by prayer and supplication with thanksgiving let your requests be made known unto God. And the peace of God, which passeth all understanding, shall keep your hearts and minds through Christ Jesus."

Phil.4:4-7

The date was Saturday, April 10, 1954. We had left Mammaw and Papaw's house late Friday evening as we had decided to drive overnight to give us more time to visit with my family. I had been driving and we stopped for something to drink. It was about 3:30 a.m. and I got a cherry coke and Jerry got a grape drink. Jerry said he would drive for a while so I could get some sleep. We started off laughing and talking and enjoying our drinks. We were excited about our future. Jerry was looking forward to going to OCS and I was looking forward to going shopping with my mother. Easter was only a week away and even though we didn't have much money, I thought I could squeeze out enough to get a new dress for Easter. Finally, when I had finished my cherry coke I decided to lie down and see if I could sleep for a while. I laid down and put my head on Jerry's knee. In a little while, I was almost asleep, I felt him lift his leg and apply the brakes. He was blowing the horn. I lifted myself up on my elbow to see what was happening and suddenly everything went blank.

Somewhere deep in my brain I heard Jerry calling my name. I remember thinking "Why does he keep calling my name, doesn't he know I am right beside him?" I tried to say something, to tell him I was there, but nothing came out of my mouth. He asked me if I was o.k. I felt something on top of me, heavy, preventing me from moving. The next thing I remember was Jerry yelling very loudly. Then I felt the heaviness on top of me releasing me, but I still couldn't seem to move. Then I began to sing. Something must have been coming out of my mouth because someone said, "Just keep on singing, little girl, keep on singing."

We had been in an accident. A young man had just gotten out of the Navy and was driving from Charleston, SC to Ohio – going home. He had been partying and drinking before leaving Charleston and fell asleep at the wheel of his car and his car had drifted into our lane. Jerry apparently saw the on-coming car and tried to avoid a collision by going to the shoulder of the road, but the other car kept coming, going off the road and hitting us head-on. Even the blowing of the horn did not wake the other driver and the result was a head-on collision.

We were on Highway 52 between Darlington, SC and Florence, SC. Because Jerry was military, the military sent a team to investigate the accident. They determined that our car was traveling about 59 miles an hour at the time Jerry applied the brakes. According to the skid marks made by our car we were traveling about 10 miles an hour when the two cars collided and both cars were on the shoulder of the road. They estimated that the other car was going about 70 miles an hour. It was as if we had hit a brick wall. They said it looked like the cars had been lined up to hit each other head-on. The accident occurred at approximately 4:00 a.m. There was very little traffic on the road at that time in the morning. The accident happened in front of a house. The house sat a good ways back from the road. The farmer who lived in the house got up at his usual time, around 5:00 a.m. When he saw the cars he called the police and hospital. The police and ambulance got there about 5:30 a.m. and by the time they got us to the hospital it was a little after 6:30 a.m. The staff was in the process of changing shifts. New personnel were coming to work.

I don't remember very much about the accident itself, or what took place during the almost 2 hours from the time of the accident until we were in the emergency room at McLeod Infirmary in Florence, SC. So, this part of the details was told to me by several different people.

The fifth miracle - Out of Body experience

The paramedic told me that Jerry was slumped over the steering wheel and in and out of consciousness. He said Jerry had apparently been blowing the horn at the time the cars hit and the pressure of his hand on the round, chrome bar had broken it cutting his arm. The end of the chrome bar entered his chest

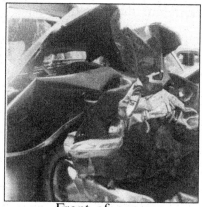

Front of our car
1954 Chevrolet

Inside of our car

penetrating it all the way through and exiting on his back penning him to the steering wheel. He said it had only missed his lung by an eighth of an inch. He said Jerry had hit his head on the top of the car causing him to have a concussion. They had to lift him off of the chrome bar and remove him from the car before they could get to me. The cedar chest had been thrown towards the front of the car, breaking the front seat loose and landing on top of me, pinning me down. When I rose up to see why Jerry was blowing the

Car that hit us

horn and applying the brakes, the cars hit and it threw me into the windshield. I hit the rear-view mirror and my face went into the windshield. The pressure of the cedar chest threw my legs into the heater which was located under the dash on the passenger side of the car. They had to remove Jerry, the cedar chest and other luggage before they could get me out of the car. He said I was singing and he encouraged me to keep on singing. He said as long as there was sound coming from me he knew I was still alive. The cedar chest broke open and everything in it was all over the car. Mother and Daddy had given me a pearl necklace for graduation and they fell out and landed in the blood from my facial cuts, and open leg wound. (The pearls turned dark and I still have them, but they are unusable because the natural color never came back.) It took about 25 minutes to get to the hospital and the paramedic said I sang all the way until they pulled into the unloading place at the hospital and then I just stopped singing. In the emergency room he said they checked me and said there was no pulse and to mark it a DOA (Dead on Arrival). They covered me with a sheet. He said it quickly spread all over the hospital about the young couple in an accident and the girl had died and it was probably better because her face looked like it had gone through a meat grinder. He said they were attending to Jerry's injuries and all he would say was, "leave me alone, take care of my wife, help her, please".

A student nurse came into the emergency room and asked if she could help. She told the paramedic she wanted to see the young girl who was killed in the accident. He took her to my bed in the emergency room and she lifted the sheet to look at me and when she did she saw I was breathing.

She screamed, "She's not dead!" and everyone immediately left Jerry and ran to my bed and started issuing orders. Almost an hour had passed since I was pronounced DOA. My parents got the call at 7:15 a.m. asking if they had a daughter named Nellie and advising them that I had been in an accident and did not survive. They were asked if they knew anyone in Florence, if so, call them. They said to tell them to come to the hospital because her husband was in critical condition.

I have relatives in Florence and so my mother called her brother and he sent his two adult daughters to the hospital. Maxine and Berlean got to the hospital about 8:00 a.m. and were told that somehow I had survived and was in surgery and they didn't expect me to live. They said that Jerry was in critical condition.

This is my personal account of what happened.

I was excited about seeing my family. I thought of going shopping with my mom since Easter was only a week away. We didn't have a lot of money, but maybe I could afford a new dress. Suddenly my thoughts were interrupted when I felt my husband put his foot on the brake pedal and begin blowing the horn. I rose up on my elbow so I could see what was wrong and then everything went black. It was several days later before I would be able to tell anyone what had happened. A car had entered our side of the road and even though my husband took every precaution possible, even going off onto the shoulder of the road, the car still hit us head-on. The impact occurred just as I rose up. It threw me into the windshield and dash. My husband was pinned to the steering wheel. Vaguely I remember my husband trying to move things (we had everything we owned in the world in the car including my cedar chest that my parents had given me for graduation) away from me and his words were comforting me, assuring me everything would be alright. I tried to talk, but only garbled sounds came forward. (Later, I realized that it must have been angels moving things from on top of me because it was impossible for Jerry to have done this since he was pinned to the steering wheel and unable to move his right arm). I was aware that I couldn't move, but I didn't feel any pain. We remained this way for a long time.

They had to remove my husband first in order to get to me. I remember his cry of pain as they lifted him off the steel bar on the steering wheel. I tried to tell him I was sorry and I loved him, but the words were only in my mind. I wanted to sing. I loved music, having studied for several years, and I wanted to sing. I began singing, and the attendants kept telling me, "Sing on, little girl, sing on."

Just as we arrived at the hospital, I stopped singing. It was so strange. It was as if I was looking at a movie, only I was in this movie. The doctors and nurses were all chattering about and I realized that they were talking about me. I looked down and I saw my body lying on a table covered with a white sheet. Their voices became clearer and they were saying things like, "Worst lacerations I have ever seen; there wasn't any way for her to survive that blow to her head; it looks like someone just smashed her foot and tried to break her leg in to; it's probably better anyway because if she lived she would probably never see, walk or be anything but a vegetable."

I heard a familiar voice. It was my husband. I looked at him lying on another table. It was evident that he was in a lot of pain. I thought about how handsome he was and how we had had so little time together. I listened and heard him say, "Leave me alone, take care of my wife. Help her, please."

The next memory I have is of being totally weightless and drifting in an upward mode. I was surrounded by the most beautiful colors I had ever seen. The closest way I can describe the colors is similar to the inside of a shell or what is called mother of pearl. The colors seem to be all around me and caressing me, comforting me, filling me with a sense of peace and tranquility. It was almost as if the colors and I were blended together. Then I felt enveloped in music. The sounds were so unbelievably serene and gave me a feeling of peace in my heart. I have never before nor since heard the kind of music that I heard at that time. It is difficult to describe because I believe it is something you have to feel to experience it and nothing on earth has ever given me that feeling.

In that instant I knew I was dead and my soul was on its way to heaven. I knew I would wake up in the arms of Jesus and it was so real. I didn't fear death because I knew that Jesus was my Savior and I had served Him and had the promise of eternal life since I was 13 years old. I welcomed and even looked forward to meeting Jesus and God and beginning my life in eternity. I eagerly looked forward to seeing Jesus. I had read about Him in the Bible, heard and knew all the stories about His three years of ministry on earth and I was excited that I would get to see all the people I had read about in the Bible.

In an instant I remembered that Jerry wasn't a Christian and I didn't want to be separated from him for all eternity and I cried out to God and asked Him to give me a little time. Time to lead my husband to salvation and then I would be ready to go. Did I see God? Did He speak to me? No, I didn't see God, but I know He saw me because I felt His presence in and through me. It was as if we were meshed together as one and I felt total peace. I knew He had heard my plea and was granting me life. The feeling was overwhelming and I sensed His arms enveloping me and comforting me and assuring me that He loved me and was giving me my request for time. In some inaudible way I understood that He loved Jerry, too, and He was sending me back to take care of what I had been too busy to take care of before the accident. I can't explain why I had not tried to help Jerry understand that he needed Jesus as His Savior. As I look back, the only excuse I have is that we were together for only short periods of time and he always went with me to church when we were together and I guess I just took for granite that since he was a good man he was saved. (So many people believe that all you have to do is be good and you can go to heaven. That is so wrong. The only way to get to heaven is to repent of your sin, ask God to forgive you and ask Jesus to come into your heart, cleanse you and make you whole. When you do that the blood of Jesus cleanses you and makes you His child.)

Of course, during this transition time I felt God instill in me what I had read in His Word and not realized the importance of it until I was in His presence. I know now that we are saved by grace, not by works, it is the gift of God. I know now that no matter how good you are or how many good deeds you do it will not grant you the privilege of eternal life. I know that no matter how much we want to share heaven with our loved ones, the only way to do that is for each person to have a personal relationship with Jesus. I could not accept Jesus for Jerry, but I could help him realize that he needed Jesus and that he needed to ask forgiveness and invite Jesus to live in his life and that he needed to commit his life to serving Jesus.

It is so strange that although I did not come face to face with God, the Holy Spirit was flowing all through my spirit and the impression of God's love was so overwhelming that I did not need to see Him to know that I was in His presence. I had heard about heaven and the streets of gold and the many mansions that had been prepared for His children and I knew that I was on the outskirts of heaven and I knew the brightness I was experiencing was the streets of gold. I was also surrounded by angels. They did not have wings, but their faces were so pure and love flowed freely as I felt them ministering to my body. It was as if they were draining all the pain and taking it upon themselves so I would not suffer.

As soon as I cried out to God I felt my spirit enter my body and it was at that moment a nurse lifted the sheet to see the girl who had been so badly injured that her face looked like she had been through a meat grinder and she yelled, "She's not dead!"

Everything stopped and there was a rush of doctors and nurses hovering about. I tried to talk but the words wouldn't come out. I still felt very strange, like I was in my body, but I wasn't in my body, but watching everything from outside of my body. It was as if I was suspended between life and death. I heard the doctor say, "let's get her to surgery." I saw them push me down a long hallway and into a room that was very bright. I heard a doctor say, "we don't have time to call a plastic surgeon and Dr. Lide is on his way." I saw them take x-rays of my entire body.

Dr. Dawson was an orthopedic surgeon and I saw him working on my foot and leg. He pushed two long steel bars through my leg, one just below the knee and one through the ankle. I watched as he said, "We can't wait; I'll stitch up her face as soon as Dr. Lide removes her eye. I don't believe she's going to make it anyway so it probably won't matter how she looks." I saw the fluid going into my arm and I wanted to tell them I was going to live because God had heard my plea and was going to give me time to witness to my husband so we would not be separated for all eternity, but it was if they couldn't hear me. Most of the handwritten copies of the doctor's notes from the hospital are faded, but some of the typed notes are still readable and the following are excerpts from those documents:

> 4-10-54 Mrs. Jerry (Nellie) Hartsoe
>
> Case No. 15, 228
>
> 61 Cypress St., Charleston, SC
>
> Age 18
>
> Diagnosis: DOA 6:33 a.m.   G. R. Dawson
>
> Patient's face horribly mutilated, - some of the most terrific lacerations I have ever seen. The globe of the left eye was ruptured.
>
> Diagnosis: Updated – patient breathed –
>
> 7:30 a.m. Rushed to surgery

The traumatic wounds of the face are prepared in the usual manner and draped with sterile drapes. Debridement is carried out and the wounds closed with interrupted fine cotton sutures. Sterile dressings are applied. Enoculation of left eye. The conjunctive was severed from the globe at the limbus. The extra-ocular muscles were isolated and severed from the globe. The optic nerve was cut 10 mm back of the globe. A glass ball was implanted into Tenon's capsule. Tenon's capsule was closed with interrupted silk sutures. The conjunctive was closed with a running silk suture. Under local anesthesia 1% procain with wydase, the leg was given the usual preparation and sterile drape off. Four 4/32´stainless steel pins were passed through the tibia, two above and two below the compound fracture and incorporated in plaster to maintain traction. The wounds were closed with white cotton. I attempted to mold the foot6 blindly and the entire leg was put in a long leg cast with the knee in 10° flexion. Closed reduction of the colles fracture under local anathesis was done. A long arm cast was applied with the hand in flexion and ulna deviation. Surgery began 8:30 a.m. and ended at 12:30 p.m. Comment: This patient will have a bad leg.

Follow-up Diagnosis: X-Ray shows rt. Colles compound comminuted fracture tibia lower mid third. Fracture tibial plateau, rt. Extensively comminuted fractures of the tarsal and metatarsals (clinical diagnosis). Fractures of right tibia and fibula. Fractures 2nd and 3rd metatarsal bones with lateral dislocation of 3rd, 4th and 5th metatarsals. Commuinuted fracture of right cuboid bone. Operation: Closed reduction rt. Leg. Insertion of pins. Application of long leg cast. Cast to right wrist.

Surgeons: Dr. H. G. Taylor; Dr. G. R. Dawson;
Dr. L. D. Lyde, Jr.

While I was in surgery, I saw my parents and the nurse was comforting them. Maxine and Berlean were there and were telling them that a nurse saw that I was breathing and they had rushed me to surgery and that they didn't expect me to survive. They told mother and daddy that they had not been able to talk to me or see me or Jerry. I tried to tell them I was o.k., but it was obvious that they couldn't see or hear me. It was as if I was there, but my physical body was not.

I was in what they called a coma for seven days. Then, as they said, I woke up. They were amazed that I could tell them what they said, what my mother wore, that when my oldest brother got to the hospital I saw him as he walked in my room, took one look at me and passed out on the floor. The reason it was difficult for them to believe me was because my eyes had bandages covering them and I couldn't talk clearly because my gum had been severed through my top lip and nose and they had pushed my top teeth back up and sown them in which prevented me from speaking clearly. They thought I had a very active imagination, but no one could explain how I knew all the details I shared.

I had one cut that ran from my forehead through my left eye, down my cheek, through my top lip and gum and stopped about two inches from my mouth on my right cheek. My right eye had a cut across the top lid and I had multiple other cuts. My right wrist was broken, my right leg was broken so badly they had to remove the small bone and put steel rods above and below the break to hold the large bone in place. The skin had to be repaired over the break. My right foot was crushed and they tried to put the bones back in place, but two of the bones were never put in the right place. My left leg had been bruised so badly that gangrene had begun. Two doctors said they needed to remove the leg below the knee before it spread. One doctor said, let's try penicillin first and see if we can save the leg. Fortunately for me he was right and my leg was saved, only years later it collapsed and they found that the ligaments had been destroyed so I wound up wearing a long leg brace for 17 years or walking with crutches or not walking at all. Getting rid of that brace after 17 years and being able to walk without it was just another of the miracles God has given me.

Jerry had a severe head injury and several cuts on his face and arms. The chrome bar on the steering wheel had broken, cutting his right arm and entering his chest penetrating it all the way through exiting on his back. It also broke his collar bone in three places. It missed his lung by 1/8 of an inch. He spent 11 months in Walter Reed Army Hospital in Washington, D. C. and lost his chance to go to OCS due to his injuries which prevented him from doing the physical portion of the training.

The young man who caused the accident received a broken knee cap, and had two teeth knocked out. He was fined $17 for driving to the left of the center line. His father came from Ohio and took him out of the hospital and back to Ohio without paying the fine or hospital bill and without being properly released from the hospital. This was two days after the accident while I was still in a "coma".

He was twenty-one, no job, and no insurance. Both cars were totaled. Daddy took our insurance money and went to the auction in Georgetown and bought us another car. People have asked why we didn't sue the man that caused the accident, but since he didn't own anything or have anything, it would have only cost us more money that we didn't have and our recovery was more important than suing someone that didn't have anything. It is also strange that we did not

The fifth miracle - Out of Body experience

know the young man's name. Neither Jerry nor I ever had negative thoughts about the young man that caused the accident. The only thing that was ever said was said a week before Jerry died. I will tell you about that later on in the story.

I thank God that He heard my prayer and let me live and for the extraordinary experiences I had. Although I wrote everything down as soon as I could write, it was several years before I shared this with anyone because when I tried to tell them things that had happened they thought it was all my imagination and people didn't talk about "out of body experiences" until several years later.

I have to tell you about a couple of things that happened while we were in the hospital.

The accident happened a week before Easter, so I told my mother, who was a stickler for having a new outfit for Easter with everything matching, that God knew Jerry and I didn't have money for new outfits so he fixed it so I wouldn't have to have a new outfit. God knows our every need and I'm sure he didn't cause the accident because of our lack of money, but I also believe that He allowed it to happen to help us realize that there are more important things than new outfits.

My room was larger than Jerry's room so after bath's and breakfast they would push his bed into my room. Since both our right sides were injured they would put his feet at my head and my feet at his head so we could hold hands with our left hands. Jerry was in a lot of pain, but I didn't have any pain during the three weeks I was in the hospital. I truly believe that while I was in the presence of Jesus that the angels I saw and felt had taken all the pain away from me and I can truly say that I did not have to take anything for pain while I was in the hospital. It had been about 10 days since the accident and the bandages were still covering my eyes. Finally, they removed the bandage from my right eye and found that the cut above the eye on the eyelid had not damaged the eye and I had sight in it. A few days later they still had not removed the bandage from my left eye.

Jerry was in my room and I could sense that something was wrong. He said, "I have to tell you something and it's hard to tell you."

I asked what it was and somehow I was afraid that they had decided to amputate my leg. I said, "Is it about my leg?"

He said, "No, it's about your eye."

I said, "Well, when are they going to take this bandage off. I'm tired of looking out of just one eye."

He began to cry and said, "It won't matter if they take the bandage off or not, you won't ever see out of that eye again."

I said, "What do you mean? If they take the bandage off, I can see out of it."

He said, "No, you won't because they had to remove the eye, you no longer have an eye there."

I said, "Well, that's no big deal. I still have one. I was afraid you were going to tell me that they were going to take my leg off."

After Jerry told me that I only had one eye and the doctor's had said I would probably never walk again without crutches, I decided to make the supreme sacrifice. Before we were married I had told Jerry that I didn't believe in divorce and if he married me it would be for keeps. I now felt that it would be wrong to hold him to someone who would be handicapped for the rest of her life so when they pushed his bed into my room the next day we had the following conversation.

"Jerry, do you remember that I said I didn't believe in divorce?"

"Yes, what about it?"

"Well, since I am not pretty anymore (my grandparent's pastor had visited me and let me see myself in the mirror and I saw all the scars, not much face left) and I may never walk again and you are young and I don't want to hold you back, so, if you want a divorce I'll give it to you."

Jerry quickly said, "Nellie, you weren't pretty when I married you so why should it make any difference now."

We have laughed over those words so many times through the years. Of course I knew he married me for my money and I never gave it to him so that's why he stuck around all those years. Ha, Ha, that's a joke, too. It took us over a year to pay all the medical bills.

He never, in almost 52 years of marriage, missed a day telling me I was the most beautiful woman in the whole world. Of course, I knew I wasn't a raving beauty, but it was wonderful to be told that I was beautiful. In his eyes I was beautiful and he proved it over and over again, but that comes later in the story.

Two weeks after the accident I was anxious to talk to Jerry about accepting Christ as His Savior. I had asked God for enough time to witness to Jerry and I didn't know how much time I had so I had an urgent feeling that I needed to talk to him about his salvation. Although I had been a Christian for several years I had not talked to anyone about how to become a Christian. God is so wonderful. He knew that I had not had that experience so He provided someone to do it for me. While I was in the hospital, my grandparent's pastor, Rev. Weathersby, came to see me several times and it was on one of those visits that I told him about my conversation with God (I didn't really know it was called an "out of body experience" at that time) and that I had asked God for time to witness to Jerry and I wanted Jerry to have the opportunity to accept Christ as his Savior. The pastor asked if it would be alright with me if he talked with Jerry about salvation. I told him it was. I didn't care who did it, I just wanted Jerry to have the opportunity to accept Christ so we would never be separated in life or in death.

It was about an hour later that Pastor Weathersby came back in my room and told me that he and Jerry had talked and that Jerry had prayed the prayer of repentance and accepted Christ as his Savior. I was so happy that I cried. I thanked God for sending the pastor and I thanked God for honoring my request for time and if He wanted to take me home I was ready to go. However, God had other plans for my life as well as Jerry's life. Jerry spent 11 months in Walter Reed Army Hospital where he had surgery and a long period of therapy to regain the use of his right arm. Jerry began to grow in his spiritual life while he was in Walter Reed Army Hospital. A year later, after being

The fifth miracle - Out of Body experience

released from the hospital, Jerry took the next step and joined my church, Rutledge Ave. Baptist Church, and my pastor, Rev. Harris, baptized Jerry in the name of the Father, Son, and the Holy Spirit.

I made a scrap book of the cards and letters we received while we were in the hospital. Also, one of the children that sang in the Cherub choir that I directed got her mother to bring her to the hospital in Florence to see us. She gave us a 3x5 card with a red rose in the center and the following prayer printed on it.

Dear Jesus,

Thank you for keeping us all through this day, for helping us work and helping us play. Now bless us tonight and all those we love, watch us and keep us, dear God from above.

In Jesus name we pray, Amen

Jerry and I adopted that prayer and whether we were together or separated, we would repeat that prayer and then add our own prayer every night. We knew that no matter where we were we were together in spirit because of that prayer and I still say it every night. It helps me to feel closer to Jerry and especially closer to God.

We were in McLeod Hospital for almost a month and then it was decided that I could either go home or be transferred to a military hospital to continue my healing process. I decided that it would be easier on everyone for me to go home with mother and daddy. A week earlier they had transferred Jerry to Fort Jackson Hospital in

Columbia and the doctors had decided that he needed to go to Walter Reed Army Hospital in Washington, D.C. since he would need extensive surgery and rehabilitation.

So, having been married less than two years and having been separated already for 13 months, we found ourselves going separate ways. Jerry went to Washington, D. C. and I went home with mother and daddy in Charleston, SC. My parents were wonderful to me. At first, my father carried me upstairs at night to my bedroom, the bedroom I had spent a number of years in while growing up. Although I only weighed 98 pounds, the cast on my arm and leg made my weight considerably more and it was awkward since the cast on my leg made my leg unable to bend so going upstairs daddy had to walk sideways so the cast wouldn't hit the wall. During the day, I was carried downstairs to the living room and placed on a roll away bed. I couldn't walk because I couldn't use crutches since my right arm was in a cast. After a couple of weeks, I decided it was too hard on daddy carrying me upstairs so I would get down on the floor and I learned to scoot backwards up the stairs and frontwards down the stairs in the morning. During the day I would lift myself up on the piano bench and make my fingers play the keys on the piano, thus exercising my fingers even though the cast on my arm covered half my hand since it was my wrist that was broken.

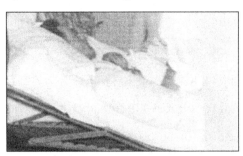
Jerry in the hospital

The fifth miracle - Out of Body experience

Jerry was busy in the hospital with undergoing surgery on his collarbone and then the painful rehabilitation to try to restore the use of his right arm and hand. He had to wear a very awkward brace that kept his arm elevated and fixed. It was his right arm and hand that was injured and he writes with his right hand, but he would get someone to write for him and just as he did while he was in Korea for those awful thirteen months, he wrote me every day. His letters were always filled with encouraging messages and words of love and what we would do when we were able to be together.

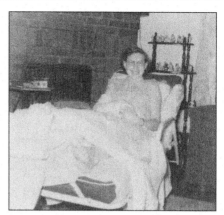
Nellie at home

Daddy and me

During the next five months, we exchanged letters and phone calls and finally, the cast was removed from my arm and it was painful learning to reuse and retrain the muscles in my hand, wrist and arm. It was during this time that I also taught my mother to drive our car. At the time of the accident we had a new 1954 Chevrolet with a stick drive. Of course it was totaled and daddy took the insurance money and bought us a new 1954 Chevrolet with automatic transmission. Mother needed to learn to drive because I had to go to doctor appointments and they were in Florence, 100 miles away and daddy couldn't always take off the time to take me. It was awkward sitting in the passenger's seat because my right leg was in a long leg cast from the foot up to my hip and I had to sit sideways in the seat so I could stretch my leg out since it wouldn't bend. Somehow we managed and as soon as the cast came off my arm, I took mother to try for her driver's license. Daddy told mother not to cry or be disappointed if she didn't pass the first time because lots of people had to try two or three times before receiving their license.

You could only try for your driver's license once a week and the place was located in North Charleston and the building was on a little incline. I drove to the station and parked the car and used crutches to go inside and wait for mother to take the written and driving portions of the test. She only missed two questions on the written test and she and the officer went outside for the driving portion. Mother got in the driver's side and the officer got in on the passenger's side. He told her to release the emergency brake and back out of the parking space. Mother looked at him and said, "Where is it?" OOPs!!! It seems that I had not told her about the emergency brake, nor had I applied it when I pulled into the parking space. Fortunately, he understood as mother told him she really needed her license as her daughter had been in a terrible accident, even pronounced dead on arrival and she had somehow survived and had to go back and forth to Florence for doctor's appointments and she really needed to be able to take her. The officer explained what and where the emergency brake was located and what it was used for.

Then he said, "Start the car, put it in reverse, and back out of the parking space."

In about 20 minutes they came back and I was relieved that mother was still driving and wasn't crying. Within the next 10 minutes they had mother's metal driver's license made and she drove us home. She had passed the test. Daddy was surprised, but kissed her and told her he was proud of her.

It was now October and Christmas was a short time away. We had so many bills from the hospital and doctors that it was difficult to pay them all. The military didn't pay for medical care for wives at that time unless it was in a military hospital or by military doctors. Our auto medical insurance paid some, but not all of the medical expenses. I still had a cast on my leg and could only walk with crutches and not very far or for very long due to the weakness in my wrist.

I called Mr. Ed who owned Edwards, Inc. I had worked for him for three years while I was in high school and then in the office during the summer after I graduated from high school and was waiting to go to college in the fall. I explained to him about the accident and the injuries we had sustained. I also told him about all the bills we had to pay. I asked him if there was anything I could do to earn some money. He said he was just opening a charge account program in all his stores and I could come in and take credit applications and he would show me how to process them. He said I could work the days and hours that I felt comfortable to work. I explained that my face was still very much unhealed and I didn't want to be a problem for people to have to look at and his reply still rings in my ears all these years later.

His reply was, "If people don't want to look at you and fill out an application for credit, then they don't deserve credit in my stores. When do you want to start?" So it was that after 6 months of healing following the accident, I went to work taking credit applications and managed to earn enough money to pay the doctor bills and have a little to buy a few presents for Christmas that year. Mr. Ed was a big, Jewish man, with an equally big heart to help others. Perhaps that is why God blessed him to finally own nine stores throughout South Carolina. Unfortunately, Mr. Ed only lived a few more years and when he died, his family decided to sell the stores and today no trace of Edwards, Inc. exists, except in my memories. I feel blessed to have known and worked with and for Mr. Ed. He taught me a lot about life and respect and how to treat your fellowman.

Jerry was able to come home for Christmas and we felt we were blessed to be able to celebrate Christ's birthday together. All too soon the holidays were over and Jerry went back to Walter Reed. This time, I went with him. Although I was on crutches, I didn't have that awful long leg cast on my leg. We found a room to rent in a home with an elderly lady. It was only a few blocks from the hospital so Jerry was able to come home every night and go back to the hospital during the day for his treatments. It was at this time that I had to have my wisdom teeth removed. The appointment was made at Walter Reed and it was decided to give me gas while they removed

The fifth miracle - Out of Body experience

my wisdom teeth. I thought I could drive home afterwards, but I was so out-of-it that Jerry had to get a special pass to drive me home. He had great difficulty trying to keep me upright since he still had his arm in the special brace and he had to drive with his left hand, but somehow he made it home with me in tow and the wonderful lady we were staying with took me under her wing and stayed with me since Jerry had to go back to the hospital. The next day, I had great difficulty trying to eat, so she made me some soup, and a wonderful grated ham sandwich with the softest bread I had ever put in my mouth. In fact, I have tried to make ham salad like she had made me and I have never been able to duplicate it. As I have said before, God is so good. He has a special knack of putting the people you need the most in the right place at the right time.

Another memorable event happened while Jerry was at Walter Reed that I want to tell you about. It was around Valentine's Day and many stars came and presented programs for the patients in the hospital. One of those stars was a singer named Johnny Ray and one of the songs he made famous was "Cry". He sang several songs including "Cry" and told several jokes/stories as part of his program. Johnny Ray was also deaf so it was especially inspiring to see that he had made a success of his life regardless of his handicap. He made such an impression on me. I can still see him on the stage performing and I still remember two of the joke/stories he told that day. (That is especially remarkable for me, since my children can tell you that I don't catch on to jokes or remember stories that someone tells.) I want to share one of these stories with you.

Twelve Miracles Including a Glimpse of Heaven

A man came to the United States from Germany. He didn't speak English. He arrived in New York City and was amazed at all the buildings and restaurants. He had heard a lot about the American Apple Pie so he decided he would go into a restaurant and order a piece of Apple Pie. He went into a restaurant, sat down and when the waitress came over to take his order he said in broken English, "Apple Pie and Coffee." The waitress wrote it down and left to go get it. The man felt very good since he had made his request known even though he didn't speak English. The waitress came back with the apple pie and coffee and the man ate every bite and then paid for it and left. Later, he was hungry so he went back to the restaurant and he just sat and listened as people ordered different things. Finally, he decided what he wanted to order. The waitress came and asked him for his order. He politely replied, again speaking in broken English "Hot Roast Beef Sandwich and Coffee." The waitress replied, "White or Rye?" He looked puzzled and repeated, "Hot Roast Beef Sandwich and Coffee!" The waitress replied, "Yes, sir, White or Rye?" He became a little bit annoyed and said with firmness in his voice, "A Hot Roast Beef Sandwich and Coffee." Just as annoyed, the waitress, with a firm annoyed voice said, "Yes Sir, White or Rye?" The man just threw up his hands and said, "Apple Pie and Coffee." The waitress returned with his apple pie and coffee.

As I tell the story now, without his antics and accent, it doesn't seem so funny, but at that time, it was like a breath of fresh air to have someone care enough about the patients that they would donate their time and talents to help patients relieve the stress of pain and suffering for a few minutes of laughter and relief. It was another way I believe that God provides for humor to relieve pain and suffering. He truly is an awesome God that meets all of our needs including humor. It has been said that laughter helps heal sometimes better than medicine.

In March, 1955, Jerry was ready to return to active duty. Of course he had been disqualified for Officers Candidate School because of his physical injuries. He was assigned to the base at Columbus, Georgia. We moved to Columbus and found a small house to rent. He began his responsibilities and I registered for school. I also took the test to become a Civil Service worker and was assigned to work in the supply office as a clerk. For the next few months we did well. I had been fitted with a long leg brace that was attached to my shoe and I either walked with the brace or I walked with crutches or I didn't walk at all.

It took me a year to learn to walk without the brace or crutches. I would practice every day. I would take the brace off and hold on to the bed and walk from the head to the foot and gradually I was able to turn loose of the bed and take a few steps on my own. I worked so hard. Jerry didn't know I was doing this. I always did this while he was at work. We also attended a Baptist church and I was asked to lead the music. It felt so wonderful to be able to use the talents God had blessed me with for His glory. We had old fashioned song services every Sunday afternoon and people would come from all around and we had solos, duets, quartets, and group singing. We truly felt alive and blessed. Jerry's mother came to live with us and we were able to pay for her to go to school to become a Licensed Practical Nurse.

We don't always understand why things happen the way they do, but we do know that God knows and He is always in control. In October, 1955, three weeks after we had just bought a new car, Jerry received orders for Germany. At first we thought I would be able to go with him, but then we were told that they didn't have quarters for us and I would have to wait a few months before I could join him. Jerry's mother had finished her school and went to stay with a friend in Chicago, and work at a nursing home there. I went home (Charleston) once again and continued with school and I worked part time with Mr. Ed.

In late November 1955, Jerry went to Heidelberg, Germany. Once again he wrote every day, but I was impatient to join him. We had been married over three years, but had only been together a few months. In December, I had another accident. A man ran a stop sign and I hit his car. It upset me very much. The police called my father and he came right away. The car was still drivable so my father made me get back in the car and drive to the doctor's office to get myself checked out. He followed me in his car. I was so scared and I didn't like my father very much for forcing me to get back in the car and drive. Much later I understood why he made me drive.

I was in for another surprise when I got to the doctor's office.

The fifth miracle - Out of Body experience

After checking me over, asking questions, and running blood tests, he announced to me that I was not physically hurt in the accident, just lots of bruises and I would probably be sore for a few days. He also told me that I was pregnant. I was so happy. We would finally have the family we wanted. I didn't want to tell Jerry in a letter and so I decided to wait until I went to Germany. Unfortunately, keeping my pregnancy a secret turned out to be a big mistake because I didn't tell the doctors at the base that I was pregnant. I found out later that had I told them I was pregnant I would have been able to fly to Germany instead of going by ship. It is sad that we try to live our lives making decisions without prayer or seeking God's guidance.

In April, 1956 I received my orders to go to Germany. I had to go to New York and leave from there to go by ship. Mother and daddy and Faye drove me to New York. We got there two days early so we were able to look around the city. We went to the Empire State Building and on the top floor they had lots of little shops. They also had a machine that you could make your own record. Daddy went in and sang his famous "First night" song and then Faye (she was 11 at the time) wanted to make a record. She wanted me to go in with her. Inside the small compartment the record machine said to begin singing. Faye had forgotten how the song went so she kept saying "How do you start it off?" "How do you start it off?" and before I could tell her how to start it off the record finished and began playing "How do you start it off? How do you start it off?" We all laughed and laughed.

The trip to Germany would take 10 days. Although I was 5 months pregnant I didn't show. I had not gained weight and when I arrived in New York they said I did not have all the shots I needed and so I had a Typhoid, Tetanus, and Typhus shot at the same time the day before boarding the ship. On the ship, there were four people to a room. The room had bunk beds and because I was the youngest of the four people I had to take an upper bunk. I had never been on a ship before and this one was huge. Of course, the first day out I found out what sea sickness was. That coupled along with morning sickness made me feel very ill. One of the ladies in the room with me told me I should go to the doctor on board and tell them I was pregnant and experiencing sea sickness and they could probably give me something to help. I was stubborn and felt that I would feel better in a day or two. I was tough. I didn't want any special treatment. The second night out we got into a terrible storm and the loud speaker came on and told everyone to put on their lifejackets and assemble on deck in case we had to abandon ship. We tossed and turned and at times I thought the ship was going to roll over on its side.

Finally, we were told that the danger was over and we could go back to our rooms and take off our lifejackets.

When I climbed back into my bunk I felt terrible. I had stomach cramps and it was impossible to sleep. The next morning I went to see the doctor because I had started bleeding and I was frightened. I had a temperature and the doctor said I had to stay in the "sick bay"

The fifth miracle - Out of Body experience

for a couple of days. He wanted to watch me. I told him I had had three shots the day before we left and he said that was what was causing my temperature and cramps. The next day, the bleeding was worse and I knew I would have to tell him I was pregnant. He was extremely upset when I told him and told me how foolish I was not to have told the officials that I was pregnant. He gave me some medicine and ordered me to stay in bed. The fourth day of the trip is one I will never forget. It was about 10 a.m. and suddenly I had the most severe cramp I had ever had. I knew I was going to have another miscarriage. I told the doctor how I felt and he told me that some women have miscarriages and that it didn't mean that I wouldn't ever have children. "After all", he said, "I could get pregnant." His words didn't give me much comfort. About 2 p.m. I lost the baby. The baby was a boy. I was heartbroken and I cried for the next two days. I had to stay in "sick bay" another three days. I don't know what happened to the fetus. I was so young and so upset I never asked what happened to the baby. I know now that someday I will meet my baby in heaven.

Finally, the day came to get off that terrible ship. Once we debarked we were loaded on trains that would take us to the different locations in Germany. Not everyone was going to the same place. When, after a few hours ride, I arrived in Heidelberg, I saw Jerry waiting for me.

I really needed him to share the loss with me. I waited until we got to our apartment before telling him I had something to talk to him about. I told him about being pregnant and not telling anyone, even him, and getting the shots, being in a storm, spending time in "sick bay" and losing the baby and that it was a boy. He was a little sympathetic but not like I thought he should be and I began to cry. I asked him why he wasn't upset and I accused him of not wanting to have a family. Once again, he was so much more mature than me. He caught me by the shoulders and said, "How can I miss something I never knew existed. Had you told me, I would have told the authorities and they would have flown you over here instead of making you come by ship."

By this time I was really crying and then he put his arms around me and held me close and said, "At least we know you can get pregnant, so we just have to be patient and follow doctor's orders from the time we know until you have the baby. We will have a family one day."

Chapter Seven:

The Sixth Miracle – Starting our Family

"And he will love thee, and bless thee, and multiply thee: he will bless the fruit of your womb, . . ."

Deut. 7:13a

*O*nce again, Jerry was right, because within a year we were blessed with our first child, a boy, but I'm jumping ahead.

We settled into our apartment and quickly made several friends. Jerry was coach of the USAR basketball team and our house became the central stopping point for the team and their families. The country was beautiful, the people were extremely nice and we were happy to be together, finally. The basketball team kept winning and we were finally at the finals for the championship. We had to go into two overtimes, but finally the last ball went through the hoop and Jerry's team had won the championship. Everyone was overjoyed and celebrate with drinks. Jerry and I were different because neither one of us drank, yet, no one put us down, or treated us differently. They respected us for our values. We had coke in our champagne glasses.

I was asked to lead the music at the chapel and I did. I also substituted as a teacher in school and taught private piano lessons. In June 1956 I had to have more surgery on my right foot. The bone that is usually on top of your foot was on the side of my foot. The foot was so badly crushed in the accident that they did the best they could to put it back together, but it gave me a great deal of pain and trouble with wearing shoes so it was decided to cut the bone off and fuse the bones in the foot together. That would allow me to wear shoes more comfortably but I would not be able to move my toes. So, once again I was in a cast from my foot and up my leg to just below the knee.

After I came home from the hospital I was pretty much confined to our apartment because we lived on the third floor and I couldn't do the stairs very well. I would be in the cast for 8 weeks. During that time, Jerry was hurrying down the stairs one day and tripped and fell and broke his knee cap and wound up in a cast from his ankle to his thigh. I had to try to get low enough to put his shoe on since he couldn't bend his leg. Everyone teased him that that was carrying love too far. They said just because I had a cast on my foot and leg it didn't mean he had to do something to put him in a cast so we would be even. Friends were very helpful doing

Nellie and Jerry in Germany with casts

The Sixth Miracle – Starting our Family

our shopping and helping around the house. One friend, the teenage daughter of the couple who lived across the hall from us, offered to come over and help Jerry put his socks and shoes on since both of us were in casts. Jerry enjoyed that offer of help. Jerry went to work, but couldn't continue to coach the basketball team. That didn't stop the gang from coming over and hanging out.

In August 1956 Jerry had to go back in the hospital and have his shoulder operated on again. This would be the second time they had to perform surgery on his collarbone. As it healed it had apparently pinched a nerve and they had to release it before it caused permanent damage. It was on our 4th wedding anniversary and he was to get a weekend pass so we could celebrate. Of course there wasn't much we could do because I still had the cast on my foot and leg and he, once again, had that awful brace on his right arm, but at least we would be together to celebrate our anniversary.

I was sitting in the car waiting for him to come out of the hospital when one of the men came out and told me that I needed to come inside because something had happened to my husband. I was really frightened. I imagined all sorts of things. I never imagined what had actually happened. When I walked in to his room his lips were swollen and looked like someone had chewed on them. He had a cut on his head and he looked like death warmed over. I asked what had happened to him and was told, matter-of-factly, that he had had an epileptic seizure. I didn't know what that was as I had never heard of it before.

The nurse explained what happened. She said Jerry was sitting at a table with another patient playing cards when he began to jerk and several people standing by tried to hold him down and he picked the nurse up with his right arm (the one that had been operated on) and threw her over the table before they finally held him down. In the process, he had torn the stitches in his shoulder and chewed his lips really bad. They had given him a shot to put him to sleep so he could sleep it off. Needless to say, we didn't go anywhere or celebrate our anniversary. We were just grateful he was o.k. He remained in the hospital two more weeks and did not have any more seizures. I thought I was just nervous about what had happened and that was what was making me so nauseated. Finally, in September I decided to go to the doctor because I was continuing to be nauseated. The doctor told me it wasn't nerves making me nauseated. I was pregnant and as far as he could determine I was about five months. He said the baby would be due in January. That would mean that I had gotten pregnant shortly after arriving in Germany.

We were both excited about becoming parents. The doctor said that I shouldn't have gotten pregnant so quickly after the miscarriage, but we should be o.k. After both Jerry and I had blood tests they told us we had the RH factor between us. Jerry's blood type was A positive and mine was B negative. They didn't advise people to have more than two children because the baby could be abnormal and that could explain why I had had two miscarriages. It seems that the baby has to feed from my blood and if the baby had Jerry's blood type it might mean that the baby would be deformed, retarded, have brain damage or be physically handicapped. It might also mean that the baby would have to have all of its blood drained out and replaced to prevent future problems. We simply said we would take our chances. Because of having a cast on my leg I couldn't be as active as I had always been and I believe that, along with God's perfect timing, is what helped me carry this baby to full term.

It was also during this time that I experienced Jerry having a seizure. Above our bed was a chain that turned the overhead light on. One night I felt Jerry's arm across my waist and it was ridged. I reached up and turned the overhead light on and I could see that he was stretching in the bed trying to keep his body from jerking and he was chewing his lips. I ran across the hallway and banged on the door to get some help. When we got back to the bedroom Jerry was on the floor under the bed. He had apparently jerked himself off the bed onto the floor. Bob (the neighbor next door) shoved the bed off of Jerry while his wife, Ethel, called for an ambulance.

I was in shock. I had never seen anything like this before and I was scared. The ambulance came and they took Jerry to the hospital. I went with them and it just seemed like they didn't really care and were not very concerned. They said he would be there a couple of days and then he could go home and back to work. I tried to ask questions, but I really didn't know what questions to ask. I felt so alone. I prayed and asked God to help me know what to do. I loved Jerry, but I didn't know how to help him.

They gave Jerry some medicine and sent him home. Everything went o.k. for a few weeks and then one morning he was sitting at the table drinking a cup of coffee when he began to jerk and hit the coffee cup and saucer and it broke and cut his hand. I pulled the table away from him and he fell on the floor. I went next door and Bob and Ethel came over and called an ambulance and once again Jerry went to the hospital. By this time I was frantic. Something terrible was happening to my husband and I didn't know what to do to help him and no one else seemed to be concerned. The news of his "fits" quickly spread through his office and his "friends" made excuses not to go on coffee breaks with him because he might have a "fit" and they didn't know what to do. Jerry began to withdraw from everything because he, too, didn't know what was happening to him. The medicine didn't seem to help and every two or three days he would have a seizure. As time passed, Jerry became more inactive. He would go to work and come home. The medicine made him extremely sleepy. He lost his appetite and also lost 40 pounds. The people who had been our friends and were constantly dropping by our apartment stopped coming over and we only had a few people who remained our friends. He was passed over twice for a promotion. They said the reason he didn't get the promotion was he was not outgoing enough. He became very depressed. I was so worried about him that I called the doctor and asked if I could come to see him about Jerry to see if there was something else that could be done to help him. The doctor told me that perhaps I needed to see him because I seemed to be overly concerned and that wasn't healthy. I told him I was overly concerned because the seizures were coming more often and he was very depressed and had lost a lot of weight. The doctor, again, said that I seemed to be overly concerned about my husband and that wasn't healthy for me, especially since I was pregnant. I said, fine, make the appointment, but we will talk about my husband, not me. I love my husband and I don't think you can measure love and concern. When I went to see the doctor, he simply dismissed my concern as anxiety due to my pregnant condition. So things continued without any improvement in Jerry's condition.

I started having false labor the middle of December. This lasted for three weeks. After feeling this way for a couple of weeks I went to the hospital about 4:30 in the afternoon. I was put in a room with three other pregnant women. I was so scared. I didn't know what to expect. I just wanted my mother, but she was a million miles away. Suddenly, a woman that resembled my mother came and stood by my bed and wiped my forehead with a cold cloth and told me to relax. She said it wasn't time for my baby to be born and when the time came, she would be there with me. The pains stopped and the next morning Jerry came to see the baby, but instead he had to take me home because I had not had the baby. I was so embarrassed that I said I'm not going back until after the baby is born.

Christmas and New Years came and no baby. On January 7, 1957 I began to have pains again and by 2:30 I had no choice but to go to the hospital. I was in so much pain. I was in a room with two other ladies and they were screaming and hollering and I was scared to death. When I thought I couldn't bear the pain anymore, the same lady that had comforted me before was standing by my bed wiping my forehead. She told me not to take any shots because anything that affected me would also affect the baby and to hold on because the baby would be born within a few minutes. Suddenly I was pushed into another room and in just a few minutes I heard my baby cry. It was the most beautiful sound I had ever heard. He was a perfect little boy and he looked exactly like his daddy. The pain I had felt only moments before was only a memory and the joy I felt was overwhelming. I feel that this is another miracle that God gives to mothers. The labor pains are excruciating, but the moment the baby is born, the terrible pain is a faint memory. How merciful our God is to bring such joy through such pain. No baby was every wanted more than my baby.

Two other babies were born that night, but Jerry didn't have to be told which baby was his. He said the baby looked more like him that day than any time since and he was so beautiful. He had A positive blood, but did not have any jaundice, did not have to have his blood transfused, and was in perfect condition. He weighed 7 pounds 12 ounces and was 21 inches long. I told Jerry about the lady that stood by my bed and wiped my head and gave me words of comfort and that before we went home I wanted to tell her how much I appreciated her kindness. Jerry went to the nurses' desk and asked about the lady and when she would be on duty. He was told that they didn't

The Sixth Miracle – Starting our Family

have anyone fitting that description working there. He came back and asked me if I was sure what she looked like and I told him yes, I was sure. He said they told him they didn't have anyone fitting that description working there. I tried to find her over the next two days and I didn't have any luck. I finally decided that I had wanted my mother so badly that I had just imaged the lady and then I knew that God had provided an angel to be with me and help me as I gave birth to the baby I had prayed so long and hard for and He had once again granted my prayer and given me a perfect little boy. In my prayers for a baby I had asked God to give us a baby boy and I would teach and train him in the ways of the Lord and just like Samuel in the Bible, if he wanted my baby, I would give him back to serve Him in whatever way He wanted him to serve. They had everything ready to do a complete blood transfusion for the baby if it was needed. They were amazed that the baby was perfect and there didn't appear to be any problems due to the RH factor. We had to stay in the hospital two more days before going home.

Life took on new meaning with a baby in the house. It was wonderful to watch our baby grow and sometimes I would spend hours just watching him sleep. Before he was born, Jerry had asked if we could nickname him Buzzy after a close friend of his in high school. This friend was probably the only close friend he had as he wasn't allowed to play sports, or participate in any after school activities because he had to go home to help with the dairy farm. His stepfather was an alcoholic and demanded that Jerry get up at 4 a.m. to help milk the cows before going to school and come home straight after school to help milk them again as well as feed them and clean up the barn. This friend, Buzzy, had been killed in a car accident and it had affected Jerry very much since he wasn't close with his mother and didn't have any other close friends. It also brought back the loss of his grandmother, the only other person he was close to in his childhood days. I said it was o.k. with me. We had already decided that if it was a boy he would be named after his father, Jerry Elmo Hartsoe, Jr. When Buzzy was six months old I found out that I was pregnant again. I was elated. The doctor was not happy as he said it was too soon and with the RH factor this baby could be in trouble. Unfortunately, in those days, they didn't have the technology to determine the sex of a baby or if anything was wrong with the fetus. All they had was blood tests.

During the next few months Jerry continued to have seizures and was again passed over for a promotion. In spite of the seizures, being passed over for promotion (It was determined that he wasn't sociable enough), Jerry continued to do an outstanding job and received several letters of accommodation. He became more withdrawn. We decided to take a few days off and go to Garmish, Germany, a recreation area, in the hopes that it would help him relax. When we returned to Heidelberg Jerry had orders to report to the hospital and he also had a promotion which had come down direct from Washington, D. C.

About a month before this I was so worried about Jerry that I finally wrote my parents and told them what was happening. I told them about the seizures and that the doctors didn't seem to be concerned and with a baby and another one on the way I was scared. I told them he had been passed over twice for a promotion. My father was friends with Mendel Rivers who was chairman of the Armed Forces Committee and he called him and told him about my letter and that he was concerned and would appreciate it if he would check into it and see what was happening and if there was any way he could help us. So, when he checked he saw that Jerry had been passed over for promotions and yet he deserved the promotion so he ordered it straight from Washington and also ordered for a complete evaluation of his condition and that was why he was ordered to report to the hospital.

After a week in the hospital they had not run any tests, nor even acknowledged that he was there. This was in October and I knew that time was running out for me to travel due to the danger of having a miscarriage. I took Buzzy and went to the Little White House (headquarters) and asked to speak to someone that could tell me what was going on with my husband. They simply told me to go home that things were being taken care of. I told them that was not good enough. I wanted to know what was being taken care of. The doctor didn't seem to know why Jerry was admitted to the hospital and didn't really seem to care. I said that I wanted some answers and if they couldn't give them to me I would call my father who would contact Mendel Rivers and I was sure that he could get some answers. It didn't take but five minutes for the Commanding Officer to see me.

He told me that an inquiry had come in from Washington wanting to know why an enlisted man had received numerous awards for outstanding work and yet had been passed over for a deserved promotion. He said the promotion was sent from Washington. He also said the inquiry demanded that a full medical evaluation be conducted and that the diagnosis was to be sent directly to him. He said Jerry would be transferred the next day to Landstul Hospital for a complete neurological workup and that as soon as that was completed we would be sent to the states to the closest base to my home so I would have help when the new baby came.

Jerry was transferred to Landstul Hospital and when they completed their workup they found that he had been given medicine equivalent to control seizures in a twelve year old, not a twenty-three year old man. This misdiagnosis had caused Jerry's condition to deteriorate faster than if he had been given the correct medication. This had gone on for over a year. They also determined that the seizures were happening as a result of the head injury he had sustained from the auto accident in 1954. He was given, what we hoped would be, the proper medicine to control the seizures, dismissed from the hospital and sent home. That happened on Wednesday, Oct. 30th. The next day they came and packed up everything we had and we left for Manheim, Germany to be sent home by air. We arrived in Manheim about 2 p.m. Buzzy had a high fever and the doctor said he had a severe ear infection and gave him a shot and some medicine to take and advised us not to take him on the airplane as it could cause his eardrum to burst and if that happened it could cause him to lose his hearing. We were in a quandary not knowing what to do. If we took Buzzy on the airplane and he lost his hearing, we couldn't bear it. If we didn't go that night at 7 p.m., we would not be able to go until after the new baby was born because it would be too dangerous for me to travel. I sat in the hotel room in a rocking chair, cradled my baby to me and prayed for an answer. For two hours I rocked and prayed. I didn't know what to do. I didn't want my little boy to be in danger and I didn't want to stay in Germany until my new baby was born. God is always with us and He answered my prayer. By 6 p.m. Buzzy's fever had become normal so we made the decision to fly home. We arrived in Charleston and my parents were there to meet us. It was Halloween and we felt like we had really been treated to be back in the states and close to home. We took Buzzy to the doctor the next day and they checked his ear and did not find any signs of any infection and his ears were in perfect condition. What a powerful, healing God we have! Jerry's new assignment was to be at Fort Jackson in Columbia, SC which was about 100 miles away from Charleston.

Jerry went to Fort Jackson and I stayed at home in Charleston until after Christmas and New Years. The first week in January we rented an apartment in Columbia and we prepared for the new baby's arrival. Jerry had saved his leave time so he could be with me and help take care of Buzzy when I had the new baby which I was sure was going to be a girl. I knew I would probably not be able to have any more children so I definitely wanted a girl. My mother told me that I would love the new baby regardless if it was a boy or girl. I told her that I knew it would be a girl because God and I had an arrangement and He knew I needed a daughter to go with my son and complete my family.

I had worked very hard to train Buzzy to use the bathroom so I wouldn't have two babies in diapers (they didn't have throw away diapers like they do today and I really didn't like to wash diapers and I couldn't afford to throw them away). My labor pains began early in the morning on February 4 and I called my mother to come from Charleston to get Buzzy as she was going to keep him for me while I was in the hospital. I finally went to the hospital around 8 a.m. and mother and daddy got to the hospital around 10 a.m. There was a problem with the baby. She had not turned and was not in the birthing position. They tried to turn her but could not. She was actually born breech birth (butt first, back up) and was born at 11:16 a.m. and weighed 7 pounds, 10 ounces and was 21 inches. We named her Terri Lynn. She was tiny featured and the first time I saw her she was primped up with her bottom lip punched out ready to cry. She had a little bit of red hair and her eyes seemed to be gray blue. She was perfect. God had again blessed us and given us a beautiful daughter. Once again they were prepared to transfuse her blood since she had type A positive blood. However, God is so merciful. She did not need the transfusion. When Jerry came to my room after seeing his daughter I asked him what he thought about his daughter. He replied that she wasn't as pretty as Buzzy. I said she is, too. She is beautiful. He quickly said, yes, she is beautiful and I love her. When Terri was one day old, my grandfather died. He was my father's father. They lived in the country with no indoor bathroom so my mother had to put diapers on Buzzy. He reverted to using the diapers so I did end up with two babies in diapers. It took me another whole year to retrain Buzzy to use the bathroom.

When Terri was three days old I noticed that she had a few pus pimples on her neck. I asked the nurse about it and she told me that they were taking care of it. Due to the breech birth I had to stay in the hospital a week. On the morning we were to go home the nurse brought me a tube of ointment and said for me to put it on Terri three times a day. She didn't tell me what was wrong. After going home Terri constantly cried and would always throw up after feeding. More pus pimples were breaking out. The ointment didn't seem to help. One week later it was obvious that something was really wrong. I took her back to the doctor and he admitted her in the hospital and said the infection had settled in both her breasts and they had to be lanced to get rid of the infection. She was in the hospital for a week and then we went home.

Jerry had taken leave time from the Army in order to help with Buzzy and the new baby and, of course, give me some tender loving care. Two days after we brought Terri home from the hospital the second time, Jerry's leave was cancelled and he was ordered to return to duty which left me with the two babies. Terri could not lie on her stomach due to the surgery on her breasts. She still cried constantly and could not tolerate milk. I chose not to breast feed and so we had tried three different kinds of milk and nothing helped. She just could not keep the milk down. When she was six weeks old I had a breast abscess and had to go in the hospital to have it lanced and since Jerry's leave had been cancelled my mother came and picked up both babies and took them back to Charleston with her. After a week in the hospital I told the doctor I had to go home to take care of my babies. He didn't want me to go as I still had stitches in my breast, but he agreed to release me. I called mother and she brought the babies to me.

Once again, Jerry put in for leave time (he had over 30 days that he could take) and his commanding officer refused to grant him leave so I had my left arm in a sling so I wouldn't break the stitches in my left breast and two babies to take care of. Buzzy began running a high fever and I knew I would have to take him to the doctor. Since Jerry couldn't take off, I loaded Terri and put Buzzy in the car and drove to the base to see the doctor. When we went in the doctor took some blood, listened to Buzzy's chest and said he had rheumatic fever. He also said his heart had an extra heart beat. He gave him a shot, gave me some medicine to give him and sent us home.

I felt overwhelmed. In anger I drove to the headquarters at Fort Jackson. I didn't know and never cared to learn anything about rank. All I knew was that my husband had saved his leave so he would be able to be home to help me and his commanding officer had refused to give him the leave he deserved and had earned. I guess I must have looked a sight walking into that building. I had one arm in a sling, carrying Terri in her carrying case and Buzzy holding onto my skirt. Someone came up to me and asked if they could help me. I said I want to see Mr. Costello (it was General Costello) and if he was busy, I'd wait.

Someone else came out and asked if they could help me. I told him I would start with him but I wanted to speak to someone who could get my husband the leave he had earned. The leave was not for pleasure, but to help me. I continued to tell him, through my tears, that if he couldn't get my husband's leave, I'd call Mendel Rivers and I was sure he could get my husband's leave approved. He excused himself and when he came back he told me that I could go pick my husband up because he was officially on 30 days leave. He also told me that they would check into why his leave was cancelled and not granted and that I needed to be aware that if he had done something wrong that would prevent his leave they would have to take appropriate action. I looked at him and said, "If you find out that he hasn't done anything wrong except to want to help his family, will you do something to the person that denied him his leave?" He told me that they would take care of the matter after they did their investigation.

I thanked him and told Buzzy to hold onto my skirt and we got in the car to go get Jerry. I had put Terri, still in her carry case, in the back seat. I put Buzzy in the front seat with me and drove to the building to pick up Jerry.

The building he was in was down a little hill and I had parked on top of the hill. Terri was crying and I got out of the car to get in the back seat to give her a bottle while waiting for Jerry. As I closed the front door and started to open the back door of the car the car began rolling down the embankment towards the building. I put my left arm (the one in the sling) through the front window and ran backwards down the hill trying to hold the car back. I'm sure it must have been a sight to see. Of course, my efforts were in vain and the car crashed into the building. Buzzy was thrown into the dash and I had torn the stitches in my breast which was now bleeding, skinned my knees and Terri was still crying. One of the men came out and checked on all of us and then he backed the car back up the hill and put it in park. I picked up Buzzy and we got into the back seat. I picked Terri up and was holding both babies close to me while bleeding from my breast and crying along with the children when Jerry came running up to the car. He had not been there when I first arrived. He looked at me and asked me if I was all right. I said, "I may never be all right again. Will they put you under the jail?" (He had always told me that he was responsible for my actions and that if the Army wanted you to have a wife and family they would have issued one.) He said, "Nothing else matters except that you and the children are o.k." Buzzy had a nosebleed, but otherwise he was just scared. Terri was not hurt. He took me back to the hospital and they re-stitched my breast and said I needed to stay in the hospital to avoid any further infection. I told them I could not stay in the hospital as I needed to go home with my babies. Jerry was on leave for the full thirty days and he was advised that his commanding officer who had refused to give him his leave time had been transferred. He was also told that he should have never been assigned to a combat unit because of his profile (epilepsy prevents a person from being around moving machinery) and he had been reassigned to the position of clearance and assignment of government quarters. Their investigation had revealed that he had not done anything wrong. His commanding officer was angry because Jerry had only been there a short time and already asking for thirty days leave and so he refused to approve the leave. The only thing we heard about the damage to the building was that it broke seven boards and the end of the building had to be replaced.

Eventually all things worked out. I can't say that I enjoyed the first two – three years of having children since so much happened. I know that no children were ever wanted more or loved more than my son and daughter. It was just doctors, diapers, and trying to keep up with two babies who constantly needed care. Buzzy's heart was damaged from the rheumatic fever and he had to be hospitalized and was placed on digitalis to help regulate the extra heart beat that was left from the rheumatic fever. Terri finally healed and was able to lie on her stomach.

We found out how lucky and blessed we were to have our daughter when she was about six months old. I ran into one of the nurses that helped take care of her in the hospital and she remarked about how beautiful she was and how lucky we were to have her. When I asked her what she meant, she said there were three babies in the nursery at the same time that had contracted the infection and unfortunately two of the babies died and Terri was the only one that survived. I asked her how come I didn't know that it was that serious and she said the hospital was afraid of a law suit for negligence and so they kept it very quiet and when I thought back to Terri going back into the hospital I remembered that we didn't get a bill and we were told that it was covered by the bill when she was born. They probably didn't bill us because it was the hospitals fault that she contacted the disease in the first place and they didn't want us to sue them. We were so thankful that God had spared our precious daughter and we felt sorrow for the parents whose children didn't survive. At this time Terri's biggest problem was finding something she could tolerate to eat and drink. Finally, we tried goat's milk and that stayed with her. Then it was giving her one food at a time for three days to see what she could tolerate. She was allergic to almost everything. The only things she could tolerate were peas and carrots and goat's milk until she was three years old.

Even with the health issues with the children, an exciting thing happened during these years. I had entered Buzzy in a contest for the most photogenic child and also as a contestant for Little Master of Columbia. It turned out that Buzzy won the most photogenic child contest and was given a large painting of him which still hangs on my wall and also a beautiful chair which he referred to as his King's chair. He also won Little Master of Columbia and was presented a

The Sixth Miracle – Starting our Family

trophy and a savings bond for $100. At the same time, I entered Terri in a baby contest and she won as the healthiest baby which we marveled at since the only thing she could eat at the time was peas and carrots and the only thing she could drink was goat's milk. When you give your children to God and trust Him with their care, it is amazing what He can do and does do to bless them.

When Terri was six months old, we bought our first house. It had three bedrooms, living room, dining room, kitchen and one bathroom. It was brick and had a small front porch. It was directly across the street from an elementary school and was the only house on that block. It cost $8,500. We paid $500 down and made payments. It was difficult because I couldn't work at the time due to the care for the children. Terri's milk cost $1.00 a can and she needed two cans a day. Jerry said he would find a part time job. He answered an ad and went for an interview. He called me and said the interview went well and the job was his if he wanted it, but the pay was commission only. I asked him what it was doing and he said it was selling family Bibles. My first thoughts were – you are not a salesman, you've never sold anything in your life, and instead of telling him that I said, "Well, it's up to you. You can do anything you set your mind too, as long as you ask God to help you." He said that the man who interviewed him told him he would teach him how to present the Bible to people. I have to admit here that I didn't have much faith in my husband as he was always so laid back and used to the military style of presentations which he did really well.

Twelve Miracles Including a Glimpse of Heaven

The man's name was Roy Title. He was a regional manager and covered North Carolina, South Carolina and Georgia. He had a strong faith and he loved music. When he would come to our house to work with Jerry he always wound up playing the piano and we would sing hymns. He played a jazzed up kind of hymn that Jerry thoroughly enjoyed. He was true to his word and he taught Jerry to be a salesman and Jerry became so good at it that within six months he was promoted to area manager and had several people working under him. He was also making more money with his part time job than with his full time military job. However, it all came to an end after about 2 years. Jerry received orders to go back to Korea.

When Terri was six months old, Jerry's mother and new husband decided to move to Columbia to be closer to us. Since she was a LPN she decided to open a licensed day care in her home. She had bought a house a couple of blocks from us and had no trouble getting a license and was immediately filled up with children to care for while their parents worked.

When Terri was three years old, Jerry's paternal grandparents (we had only met them once before) called and asked if they could come and stay with us and would we take them to a healing meeting that Oral Roberts would be holding in Columbia. Of course we told them they could stay with us and we would be glad to take them to the meeting. It seems that Granddaddy Fisher (which is the name of Jerry's biological grandfather) was the pastor of a Church of God in North Carolina. They came and we enjoyed the visit. On the night we

The Sixth Miracle – Starting our Family

took them to the healing meeting, which was held at the fair ground in a large tent, we stayed with them. The message was very good, but being good Baptists we were not used to people praying and shouting at the same time the message was being presented. Rev. Roberts told how he had been given up for dead and God had healed him and allowed him to use his right hand as a point of contact to help people receive healing from God. He never said he could heal, but only that God allowed him to use his right hand as a point of contact. We saw people walk up on the platform using crutches and after prayer and Rev. Roberts laying his right hand on the people they threw the crutches down and walked without them. At one point in the service he said, "I'm going to pray for people with allergies, severe allergies, I feel that someone is here that needs healing from food allergies. If you are that person or know someone with food allergies put your hand on them as a point of contact and pray and believe that God will heal them." At that point I put my hands on Terri's chest and Jerry put his hand on her back and we both prayed that God would heal our little girl and she would be able to eat and live a normal life. Terri could only eat peas and carrots and drink goat's milk without breaking into hives and an awful red rash.

When we got home that night, I gave Terri a glass of chocolate milk which I knew she was allergic to. She drank the milk and we waited. In my heart I knew that God had answered our prayers and so I tested my faith by giving her something I knew she couldn't tolerate. BUT, she did tolerate the chocolate milk and from that day until now she can and does eat anything she wants to eat. I praised God then and still do for I know He healed her food allergies that night.

When Jerry received orders to go back to Korea we realized we could not go with him and he would be gone for 13 months once again. Mother had given us a 6 week old Chihuahua when Terri was 6 months old. We named her Duchess. She was about 4 years old when Jerry had to leave to go to Korea. When Jerry started to leave he picked Duchess up in his arms and held her face and told her that he had to leave and he wanted her to look out for the family while he was gone. Then he put her down and she followed him to the door. About a week after Jerry left, I noticed that Duchess was not eating or drinking. I tried to encourage her, but she would not eat or drink. I waited another couple of days and she still was not eating or drinking so I took her to the vet and he asked if someone in the family had died or left and I told him that my husband had to go to Korea and he had left about 10 days earlier. The vet said that Duchess, like a lot of chiwuawuas, must have been attached to him and she was grieving for him and had contracted pneumonia and probably would not recover but he would do all he could. So I left Duchess with the vet and told the children that she was very sick. Two days later he called to tell me that Duchess had died and asked what I want him to do. I gave him permission to dispose of her body. I didn't want the children to have to go through doing something with her. So in less than two weeks we had a father and husband that had to leave us and our pet had died.

The Sixth Miracle – Starting our Family

During this time I was also serving as music and youth director at Calvary Baptist Church. It was my faith, my music, my friends, a letter from my husband (he wrote everyday he was away, just as he had done the first year we were married) and the love of my children that helped me make it through those 13 months.

Since Jerry was going to be gone for 13 months it meant that our income would be cut short so I decided to try and get a teaching position. Again, I understood what it meant to be a soldier's wife. They said that they couldn't afford to hire me because I was subject to be transferred when my husband received orders to go somewhere else, but I could substitute. So I substituted and I also did contract secretarial work. One of the contract secretarial jobs I did was to do the monthly billing for an Exterminating Company. There were two other small businesses in their building. Both businesses only had the owners and they needed someone to type letters and fill out contracts and send out bills once a month. The telephone was answered by an answering service. So between the three businesses and substituting we were able to pay our bills and have a little to put in savings. I was lucky, my mother-in-law had a licensed day care in her home and she took care of our children. I paid for their care, but it was comforting to know that my children were being cared for by their grandmother and they were also exposed to learning new thing, playing and sharing with the other children.

The policy for children to attend school was that they had to be 5 before September 15 in order to enter kindergarten. Since both my children had birthdays after that day I decided that I didn't want them to wait. Private kindergartens would accept children who didn't meet the deadline for public schools so I enrolled the children in Bates Private School. Buzzy went first and then the next year Terri went to kindergarten and Buzzy entered the first grade. They both did well and passed. By this time Jerry had returned home and was assigned to Fort Jackson doing the same job he did before he left – clearing and assigning family housing.

Things settled down and we were doing well. A few months after Jerry returned home from Korea I began having problems with my eye prosthesis. It was determined that I had developed an allergy to the ball they had placed in my eye when it was removed following the automobile accident on April 10, 1954. I needed to have eye surgery to remove the ball and replace it with a glass ball. Two of the businesses that I did letter writing and billing for moved to a small office on Hampton Street and asked me to work in the office in the mornings while the children were in school. On one occasion when I had an infection in my eye, the prosthesis had to be removed and my eye was covered with a bandage. I wrapped the artificial eye in a Kleenex and placed it in a small black change purse inside my pocketbook. I returned from the doctor's and placed my pocketbook under the edge of the desk in the office and walked next door to speak to the girl there. I was only gone a few minutes, but when I went back to my office; there were two young boys in the office. I immediately thought about my pocketbook under the edge of the desk. I asked them what

The Sixth Miracle – Starting our Family

they wanted and they replied they were looking for work and wanted to know if we needed someone to clean the office. I told them that we already had someone to do that and they turned and walked out the door. I went to check on my pocketbook and I was relieved to see that it was still there. I opened it to check to see if my billfold was still in it and it was, but the small black change purse that held my artificial eye was missing. My first thoughts were for my missing eye, but my second thought was this, "I would have given anything to have been there when those two little boys opened the change purse expecting to see money and unwrapped the Kleenex and found an eye staring at them." I'll bet they didn't steal anything else. As humorous as it was, it was also devastating because now I didn't have a prosthesis and I would have to keep the bandage on my eye until I could have another one made. Surprisingly, our home owners insurance agreed to pay for the replacement. It cost around $500 because I had to go to Walter Reed Army Hospital in Washington and stay for a week. The eye is handmade and it takes 5 days from start to finish. It was decided that since I had to go anyway, I would go ahead and have the surgery to exchange the mesh ball for a glass ball to be implanted in my eye socket. In May 1964 Arrangements were made and I went to Walter Reed Army Hospital in Washington, D.C. to have the surgery.

Several weeks after I came home from having eye surgery and a new prosthesis made, I was still experiencing periods of nausea and I finally decided to go to the doctor. Jerry went with me. A couple of years after Terri was born, I had another miscarriage and was told that I would no longer be able to have another child for two reasons. First, I no longer ovulated so I could not get pregnant and, second, due to the RH factor, it would be too risky to have another child even if I could get pregnant. We were not unhappy about that because we had a son and a daughter and felt our family was complete. During the examination the doctor said (in a very loud voice) "My God, Nellie, you are pregnant!", to which I replied, "You said I couldn't get pregnant!", and he replied, "I know what I said! But, you are about 5 months pregnant." I was in shock.

When I walked out into the waiting room I looked at Jerry and I said, "Did you hear what he said?"

Jerry said, "Everybody in here heard what he said."

I looked at Jerry again and I said, "What are we going to do with another baby?"

Very calmly, Jerry replied, "The same thing we did with Buzzy and Terri. Get a baby crib, diapers and prepare to get up all hours of the night."

At this time, I was still substituting at school, working some mornings at the businesses, directing music at church and serving as youth director, being a mom and a wife. I really felt blessed after the initial shock because I had always wanted four children, but I had been happy with the two we had. Now I felt that God was saying, "You've done well so far, I'll add to your blessings with another child."

It seems that at this time God also wanted to teach me two valuable lessons. The first lesson was very personal and brought about,

The Sixth Miracle – Starting our Family

what I hope, was responsible for a change in my attitude. Jerry was taking a lot of medication to control his seizures and it just seemed to me that he gave everything he had to his military responsibilities and very little to his family. Because of my leadership roles at church, I felt he should attend church with me. However, he usually didn't want to get up and go to church on Sunday morning. He would go on Sunday evening and Wednesday night, but he just couldn't seem to wake up on Sunday mornings and I would get very angry and say unkind things to him and usually go to church with the children and leave him at home. I'm sorry to say that I am sure he didn't see Jesus' attitude in me.

One morning (rare, because I was usually subbing or at the office) I was at home when "Moments with God" came on TV. I truly feel that God intended for me to see this program at this particular time in my life. The pastor bringing the message began talking about having a Christian attitude every day, everywhere we found ourselves. He said that a lady in his church who was very active in a lot of different areas and everyone thought was the perfect example of how a Christian should act came to him and told him she was upset that her husband wasn't a Christian and she asked him to talk with him. The pastor said he agreed to talk with her husband and he did. When he talked with her husband, her husband had this to say,

"Pastor, I love my wife, but the woman you see is not the person I see when we are at home. Her attitude is very hateful and she is difficult to deal with sometimes and if that's what Christianity is all about, then I don't need it."

The pastor thought about what the husband had said and decided to tell the woman what her husband had said. He told her that the woman people saw at church wasn't the woman her husband saw at home and that her attitude was actually keeping her husband from becoming a Christian. The woman thanked him and over the next few months, she prayed for guidance and patience and wisdom and understanding to show her husband a true Christian attitude. She never told her husband that she knew what he had told the pastor.

Several months went by and each week she would ask him if he wanted to go to church and when he replied no, she smiled and said she loved him, but did not fuss at him or belittle him for not going. One Sunday morning when the invitation was given, the woman's husband walked down the aisle and told the preacher he wanted to accept Christ as his Savior and live for Him. The preacher asked him what changed his mind. The man replied,

"The God that changed my wife into the woman she is today is the God I want to be in my life."

I sat there and knew that the message was for me. I was the woman and although Jerry had accepted Christ as his Savior three weeks after the accident, he had not become very active in attending Church and I had been less than understanding about his medical condition which was the primary reason he didn't get up on Sunday mornings to go to church. (Many years later, I now understand that he forced himself to get up every morning at 5 o'clock to do his job with the military that was supporting us and the only morning he could sleep late was Sunday and physically his body needed that rest. At that time, I didn't understand what a toll the medicine was doing to his body and how hard he was trying to cope with the changes that had resulted in a debilitating disease that he had to fight to control every minute of every day. You could see my injuries as a result of the accident, but his were hidden from view, but more real than mine would ever be. I just wish it hadn't taken me so long to finally understand what a special person he was.)

I continued to wake him on Sunday morning, but when he turned over to go back to sleep, I just said, "I love you" and took the children and went to church and said a prayer asking God to help me change and show His love every day, everywhere I went.

During this time, while pregnant with our third child, God taught me another valuable lesson. I was still working a couple of days a week in the office downtown and since we could only afford one car, I rode the bus downtown and back home. One day I was on the bus heading home and I was sitting on the side seat behind the driver close to the front door of the bus when a lady from our church got on the bus. She sat across the aisle from me. She was on the youth committee at church and I worked closely with her since I was music and youth director. She had three children. I didn't speak to her although she looked straight at me. She didn't speak to me. I felt that since I was already on the bus when she got on it was her place to speak to me first. After all, I was music and youth director and she was only a committee member. We rode several blocks in silence until we reached her stop. She got up and left the bus. I was upset because she didn't speak to me. (Remember, I was still working on my attitude and boy was God giving me opportunities to improve my attitude.) Later that evening I told Jerry about the woman and complained that she never spoke to me. He just looked at me and said, "Well, did you speak to her?"

I knew that I had not tried to speak to her or even smile at her. He was not sympathetic to my complaint. I actually forgot about it. God wasn't going to let me off that easy. Remember He was really teaching me how to grow in my Christian characteristics during these days. About 6:30 the following morning the phone rang. It was our pastor, Rev. Thomas. He asked me to go to the woman's home (the one on the bus the day before) and help with her children. It seems that when her husband got up to get ready to go to work he found his wife in the bathroom and she was dead from an overdose of sleeping pills. She had left a note saying why she had committed suicide. It seems that the day before she had gone to see her doctor and he had told her that her cancer had progressed to the point that she only a few weeks to live and because she didn't want to put her family through watching her slowly die she had decided to spare them and take her own life. She added that she had asked God to forgive her and she believed He understood her reason to take the drastic action of taking her own life and she looked forward to waking up in Jesus' arms and would see them again in heaven.

I hung up the phone and told Jerry what had happened and I cried. I was crying, not only for her family, but for my selfishness of complaining that she didn't speak to me on the bus. I had to ask myself some hard questions that I knew would never be answered. I wondered if I had spoken to her when she got on the bus, would it have made a difference in her decision. Of course, I will never know, but from that time until now, I do not wait for someone to speak to me first, I am eager to be the first to say hello.

When Buzzy was ready for the fourth grade and Terri was ready for the third grade we decided to switch them to public school. The public school was across the street from our house and it would be easier and cost less to register them for public school. Shortly after school started the principal called and wanted to talk to Jerry and me. She felt that Buzzy, while achieving at top level academically, did not seem to be adjusting socially. Most of the children in his room were 1 to 2 years older than him and he didn't seem to be on the same maturity level with them. She also had a problem with the fact that Buzzy had been in private school and this was his first time attending a public school. She was suggesting that he be placed in the third grade with children more his own age. I told her his sister was in the third grade and that would put him in the same grade with her and I didn't feel that was in his best interest, especially since he was at the top of his class academically. She asked if I would agree to have him tested at the University. I agreed and said we would abide by what they suggested. He was tested and we were told that his IQ was 160 (borderline genius) and that the only thing they could find him weak in was his ability to concentrate. If he knew he had to be accountable he was, but if in the course of conversation you stopped and asked him to repeat what was just said, he had difficulty doing it. They didn't think that was enough to hold him back in school. (We know now that this condition is called ADDHP and can be treated – but no one had even heard of it at this time.) Even with this report, the principal still insisted that a change needed to be made and they had a class that was considered third-fourth grade combination and suggested he be placed in that class so he would be with children more his own age and yet be able to achieve fourth grade level work. She said she would explain it to him so it wouldn't be like he was being held back.

Our third child was supposed to be born in September and here it was October and still no baby. I refused to go to the doctor until I was at a point where I could not walk. Jerry insisted that I go to the doctor. He felt that something was wrong and wanted me to be checked. When we got to the doctor's office, they sent me straight to the hospital. I had developed a blockage and we were in trouble. They gave me a saddle block and delivered my baby who was born back up. I was conscious and I kept asking if it was a boy or a girl and if the baby was alright. The baby was so fat and the doctor said they had to roll back the layers to see if it was a boy or a girl. Finally,

The Sixth Miracle – Starting our Family

they said it is a beautiful, healthy boy. He weighed 9 pounds and 11 ounces and was 21 inches long. The doctor said he was actually a 10 month baby and due to the blockage I had I would never have been able to have given him life the natural way. Again, God helped with this baby because he had A positive blood and they were prepared to transfuse him, but did not have to do so as he did not experience any problems. He was perfect. When he was only a few hours old he drank 8 ounces of milk. The doctor said to give him baby cereal when he was 3 weeks old. He was such a beautiful baby. He had reddish blond hair and blue eyes. He was our unexpected bundle of joy. We were so grateful to God for giving us this baby to add to our family. Buzzy and Terri welcomed the baby. We had discussed names for boys and girls before the baby was born. We had toyed with Gary Alan if it was a boy and Diana if it was a girl. We thought about the fact that we had Jerry, Jerry, Jr., Terri, and now adding a Gary. My mother had suggested that we name the baby Steven Michael if it was a boy. She said he was a gift from God and naming him after people in the Bible would be our way of saying thank you to God for His gift to us. When we were in the hospital Jerry had to go register the baby and he said on the way to the office he kept saying Jerry, Terri, Gary, and when he got to the office and they asked for the baby's name he just simply said Steven Michael Hartsoe.

Several months later, Jerry received orders for Germany. When he received orders we were told that housing was available so we sold our house in preparation for going to Germany. Another lesson was learned during this time. That lesson was that the Army doesn't always keep its word. After we had a contract on our house, we received information that housing was not available and it might be six months to a year before housing would be available. We tried to break our contract on the house. Since we would need to wait before going to Germany we didn't want to sell the house. The people who wanted to buy our house didn't want to break the contract so we had to go ahead and sell the house and that meant we would have to find somewhere to live until we could go to Germany. Fortunately, they had built several new houses in our area and we bought a house just a few doors from our house. Lots of things were going on at the same time, new baby, children switched from private to public school and the principal wanting to hold Buzzy back which would put him in the same grade with his sister, moving to a new house, and Jerry leaving, again.

While waiting for housing in Germany, Steven had a really bad accident. He was toddling around in the den and fell. He had a tinker toy in his mouth and fell on his face pushing the tinker toy down his throat tearing the back of his throat. Buzzy came into the kitchen pushing Steven in front of him. He had his hands on his shoulders guiding him to me. I was talking with my mother on the phone and turned to see why Steven was crying and all I saw was my baby with blood coming out of his mouth. Buzzy said he fell on a tinker toy. I hung up the phone without saying goodbye, grabbed a towel to put over Steven's mouth, told the kids to get in the car, and we took off for the hospital at Fort Jackson. I know I was breaking the speed limit, but I didn't care. My baby was hurt. A police car pulled in behind me flashing its lights, but I didn't stop. He pulled beside my car and yelled, pull over. I pulled over, opened my door, and yelled, "My child is hurt, I 'm on my way to the hospital. If you want to give me a ticket, follow me." I slammed the door shut and took off. The policeman followed me until I reached the gate to enter Fort Jackson and then he turned off. When we got to the hospital they rushed Steven in the emergency room and quickly got the bleeding stopped. After checking him they said he had torn the back of his throat, but they couldn't put stitches inside his mouth. They told me he would be sore and it would be hard to swallow, but the mouth and throat have unique abilities to heal themselves very quickly. They gave him a shot and we went home. They were right about the healing, because in a few days it was as if nothing had ever happened. We did notice that from that point on Steven seemed to have a deeper voice. We figured he had taken after his daddy because Jerry had a very deep, harsh voice. Steven sang bass when he was in kindergarten.

Passport Picture

Time passed and we found ourselves in Germany. I had tried to prepare the children that the dress, customs, food, and language would be different than what they knew. The first night we were there we walked from the housing area to the theatre. Our furniture had not arrived so we had to make do until it arrived. That night walking back to the apartment, Terri said, "Moma, you were right. Things sure are different over here. They don't even have any stars."

Our three years in Germany were some of the best years we had together. Since we didn't have all the things to distract from family time (no TV, fast food, etc.) we did everything as a family. I became a certified Red Cross First Aid Instructor, and a Trainer of Girl Scout Leaders as well as head of the Girl Scouts in Crailsheim, Germany. I also taught school and private piano and voice lessons. Buzzy was a Boy Scout and Terri was a Girl Scout. Jerry's commanding officer was head of the Boy Scouts and he and I often argued because I felt they showed partiality to the Boy Scouts and I fought for equal rights for the girls.

I was teaching a first aid class and my husband's commanding officer was taking the class. My husband had always told me he was responsible for me. I have to say although my husband spent 20 years in the military I never conformed to being a soldier's wife. I never learned or paid attention to rank and I treated everyone the same. We were putting together a first aid kit that you could carry in the car. As they made suggestions I listed the items on the blackboard. My husband's CO said, "How about some Jim Beam." (Jerry and I did not drink and everyone knew and respected us for our decision not to drink.) I said, "Well, I guess you can use a light at night", and I turned and wrote down Jim Beam on the blackboard. Everyone laughed, but I didn't know why until later. When we took a break for coffee and donuts, the CO walked up to me, put his hand on my shoulder and said, "Nellie, I sure hope if we're together and have an auto accident, we have some Jim Beam in our first aid kit."

I, in my dumbness of alcoholic drinks, said, "I hope so, too."

Jerry was standing there and he leaned over and said, "Nellie, Jim Beam is a brand of whiskey."

I smiled and said, "We can always use it to sterilize a wound or a medical instrument."

Again, everyone laughed – some at me, some with me.

On another occasion I was teaching a first aid class to the girl scouts and we had made a dummy to practice artificial respiration. As I was demonstrating how to use the dummy to perform artificial respiration I kept saying artificial insemination. I noticed Jerry in the back of the room waving his hands at me. It was annoying when I was trying to teach the girls a serious skill. Afterwards I asked him what he was doing and I felt terrible when he explained he was trying to let me know that I was saying artificial insemination when I should have been saying artificial respiration. At the same clinic, later on, Jerry was teaching knife safety when the knife slipped. He cut his hand and had to go to the hospital for stitches. Needless to say, those are some memories that will stay with us for some time. I also took 16 girls on a military bus to Switzerland to the Girl's Scout Chalet. It was quite an experience. We set up tents on the side of a mountain in the pouring down rain, almost slipped off a mountain in the bus as the roads were very narrow, and had our devotions in the outhouse (bathroom). We shared singing songs with the girl scouts from Switzerland.

While in Germany we went on a vacation and drove and camped in several countries. While in Venice, Italy, we rode in a gondola (the gondolier was supposed to sing to us, but he only yodeled a little – not very romantic like the pictures say it is). They had lots of small shops by the water and in one of the shops I saw a beautiful peacock figure and I really wanted it. It was blue and had spun gold in the base. Since I didn't speak Italian, I had my translation book and began to bicker with the shop keeper trying to get him to lower the price. He lowered it a couple of times and then would not go any lower. I thought if I walked away he would lower it one more time. I was wrong. He did not go any lower. I really wanted the bird, but I didn't want him to know he had won so I gave Jerry the money and told him to go buy the bird for me. He did and it is one of my prized possessions.

While we were in Chrailsheim I also directed the music at the chapel and Jerry and I started Bible classes for the children and youth in the community. I wrote and directed an Easter Cantata which was held in the theatre on post and attended by over 400 people. I also had the privilege of serving as President of the Chapel's Women's Organization; was listed in Who's Who Among Young Women, and nominated for Outstanding Military Wife of the Year.

In spite of all of these things, we managed to have quality family time. We would read and study the Bible, the children learned Bible verses and had contests on who could put a puzzle together the quickest. Buzzy, somehow, always managed to finish his puzzle first. We played all kinds of board games and also had music in our home.

In some ways I feel a little guilty about the quality time we had together as a family during those three years. The summer before Jerry received orders for Germany, we had to take Buzzy to Walter Reed Army Hospital in Washington for a heart evaluation. We decided to take a few extra days and go to New York (the World Fair was in New York at the time) as part of our trip. Just before we got to New York we received a call that my father had had a stroke and was in the hospital. We decided to go on to New York and we called Walter Reed and they moved Buzzy's appointment up two days earlier and we only spent one day in New York and then on to Walter Reed where they said he would always have the extra heart beat, but should be able to lead a normal life. The biggest problem was shock. When the extra beat occurred it would scare Buzzy and he would freeze up causing the blood not to flow properly and it would be necessary for him to learn how to control the freezing up because it could lead to a heart attack. We worked really hard to help him understand that he was not in danger and how to relax until his heart returned to normal rhythm.

We returned home, left the children with Jerry's mother and went to Charleston to check on my dad. On the way to Charleston, it was raining and as we rounded a curve in the road the back end of the car slid around. We hit one of the roadside posts, slid down an embankment and ended up in a little wooded alcove as if we had backed down the hill into that spot. Neither of us were hurt, just frightened. A car stopped and had a husband, wife, and two teenage sons. The man, his two sons and Jerry got behind the car. I got in the driver's side. They pushed; I drove the car back up to the top of the hill and back onto the side of the road. The emergency brake had locked and Jerry had to go under the car and disconnect it in order for us to go on to Charleston. As luck would have it, a policeman drove up as Jerry was disconnecting the brake and because we had a dent in the door, he decided we had been driving too fast for conditions and gave us a ticket. No offer of help, but he rewarded us with a ticket. We were just glad it wasn't any worse than it was. Again, we know that God was with us because it could have been a lot worse than just getting a ticket and some minor car repairs.

When we got to the hospital we found out that daddy needed to have surgery on his carotid artery. The surgery was scheduled for the next week. I went down and stayed with daddy the night after his surgery. He had three additional strokes during the night and never spoke another word except "No". I was torn between going to Germany and helping with my father. My sister said they would give up their home and move in with Mother and Daddy and she would take care of Daddy and her two little ones while mother went to work. So it was decided that my family would go on to Germany and we would send money to help with expenses. My sister weighed about 250 pounds when we left to go to Germany. When we returned three years later I walked past her in the airport. She had lost so much weight I didn't recognize her. It really took a toll on her having to care for our invalid father and her two small children. As soon as possible we helped them get another house and helped make other arrangements for daddy's care. Money helps, but you can't put a price on the physical, mental, spiritual, and emotional challenges a situation like this places on an individual. I will always be grateful that she made the sacrifice so I could be with my family. My father lived ten years.

When we came home from Germany, Jerry had orders for Viet Nam. Although his physical profile stated that he was not to be assigned to war areas or areas with moving machinery due to his epilepsy, he was prepared to go and do his duty. One reason he decided to go is because he had several years earlier decided that remaining in the military was the best decision for his future and for our family's future. At the time I was not happy with that decision because it seemed he was away from us more than he was with us. We had a few weeks to get settled in before he had to leave. Once again we had to say goodbye. When he got to California they offered him a medical discharge rather than going to a combat zone. At this time he had only 2 years to go to retire and he decided he would take his chances and go to Viet Nam rather than giving up 18 years of his life and not receive his retirement.

Once again we were back to writing letters. I did secure a teaching position as some of the rules for the school district had changed. Buzzy and Terri were in middle school and Steven was in the first grade. Three months after Jerry left I received a letter from him stating that they could not get his medication in Viet Nam and the doctor wanted to write the prescriptions, send them to me to get filled and then for me to send them to Jerry in Viet Nam. In the meantime they were giving him something else that they had tried before and he was not able to tolerate. He began to have seizures regularly due to not having the proper medication. By the time they sent the prescriptions to me to get filled, there had been several strong bombings and somehow they could not find Jerry. He was missing. The Red Cross tried to locate him and the military was also trying to locate him. Three agonizing months would go by without any word as to whether he was alive or dead. Finally, I got a phone call from Jerry, himself. He was in a hospital in Japan. On one of the nights when they had received heavy bombing, he had a seizure and was put into an ambulance and transported along with several others who had been injured in the bombing and sent to Japan where he contracted malaria and was in and out of a coma and no one bothered to report where he was. When he finally regained awareness he realized that we may not know where he was since he had not heard from us at all and he asked to call me to let me know that he was alive. I consider this another one of God's miracles for us. So many did not make it back from Viet Nam or if they did they had severe impairments. I am grateful that even though it was a traumatic time in our lives, I knew God was in control and He would see us through whatever we had to endure. I spent several hours in prayer thanking God for our miracle and that Jerry would soon be home with us.

The Sixth Miracle – Starting our Family

Since Jerry didn't finish what they classify as a tour of duty, within in six months of his coming home he was back on orders for Germany. At this time, he only had less than two years to retire. If we had elected to go with him he would have had to re-enlist for another four years and neither he, nor I, wanted that so we made the decision to stay put and let him go alone to Germany.

In my opinion, sending Jerry to Germany was an expense on the military and on our family that was totally unnecessary. Usually tours to Germany are for three years. Since it takes several months to discharge someone who is retiring, this meant that Jerry would only serve less than half of the tour to Germany. Once again we found ourselves saying goodbye. At least this time he was not going to a war zone.

When Jerry came home from Germany he was sent to Fort Gordon, Georgia to be evaluated for retirement. While he was there one of the tests they did required them to inject Jerry with a fluid that would allow them to see how the blood flowed through his body. When they injected him his blood pressure dropped to zero and he was tentatively dead. They had to shock him and give him an antidote to bring him back to life. They told him not to ever eat fish or anything that had iodine in it as he was apparently allergic to it.

God sure has blessed our family over and over again with miracle after miracle. Jerry retired with seventy percent permanent disability. He was so confident that he could get a job because he had 20 years experience. Since he was unable to finish and graduate with his class when he was seventeen he had taken courses and obtained his GED shortly after enlisting. He tried many places to secure a job, but because of the epilepsy the answer was always our insurance will not allow us to hire you because of your illness. He became very despondent so I suggested that he go to school.

He finally obtained a job as head custodian for a school. When he called me to tell me he had been offered the job as head custodian he apologized. I him what he was apologizing for. He said that since I was a teacher in the district he didn't want to embarrass me by being a custodian. I told him it was an honest job and I would never be embarrassed about it. It was very hard work because he was not one to let others do the job. He helped with everything necessary to maintain a clean school environment. When I went by the school one afternoon I found him drenched in sweat while mopping the floor and I knew that physically he could not continue this work. I almost insisted that he enroll and go to school. After all, he was still a young man and had many years to work after finishing college. He went to Midlands Technical College and then transferred to USC. Two years later he was contacted by Richland School District One and offered the position of Assistant Transportation Supervisor for the Dreher High School area. He accepted the offer, but continued going to USC. He kept the School position for 16 years and then he was forced to retire due to advancing medical reasons. He never missed a day of work in those 16 years. When he retired in 1989 they gave him a lovely retirement party and since he was a coin collector, they gave him 16 silver dollars dated for each of the sixteen years he had worked for the District. He continued going to college and when he finally stopped he only lacked 6 hours (2 math classes) to complete the requirements for his Degree in Education.

Chapter Eight:

The seventh miracle – Stroke – Learning to walk again at age 38

"And the prayer of faith shall save the sick, and the Lord shall raise him up; and the Lord shall raise him up; and if he have committed sins, they shall be forgiven him. . . . and pray one for another, that ye may be healed. The effectual fervent prayer of a righteous man availeth much."

James 5:15

In February 1973, my left leg gave way as I was walking down the steps at the school district's office and when I went to the doctor I was told that due to the injuries and the gangrene I had in 1954, the ligaments in my left leg had deteriorated and I would need to wear a long leg brace to help with walking.

In May of 1973 I began to have difficulty in using my right arm and hand. In the middle of my right forearm I had a sharp pain that was constant. The doctor said it was probably arthritis. It got so bad that I could not pick anything up with my right hand. One morning I felt a sharp stabbing pain in my head and I passed out. My neighbor called an ambulance and they rushed me to the hospital where they said I had suffered a stroke and it had affected the right side of my body. It was determined that I had a blood clot in my right arm (which I understand is very rare) and it moved and ended up in my brain causing the stroke. The clot was located in the left side of the brain. My right side was paralyzed and my speech was garbled. They gave me medicine to reduce the clot. They told me that I may face more TIAs or stokes in the future. It took three months of intense physical therapy before I could use my right hand and arm or walk. I would make myself lift my right arm and place it on the piano and force my fingers to move to play the keys. Since my right leg would not move, I had to use crutches with an arm rest for the right arm in order to walk. My larynx was left partially paralyzed and swallowing or talking was difficult. I stood in front of the mirror and practiced moving my lips to form words. I went to physical therapy 4 times a week for over three months. They said it was unusual for someone to have a stroke at 38, especially from a blood clot in the arm. Here again, God took over and I regained 99% restoration to the right side of my body. I regained the ability to speak clearly, but still, today, have some difficulty in swallowing and talking. To me this was another miracle that God had given me. Strokes run in my father's side of the family. My grandfather had a stroke when I was a child and was in a wheelchair for several years before he died. My father had a stroke and was confined to bed or wheelchair for 10 years before he died. He could not talk and the only word we could understand was "no" and he said it for everything. My mother had such a struggle to try to understand what he was trying to say. After another summer of active rehabilitation I was grateful that I could resume teaching in the fall of the year.

Chapter Nine:

The Eighth Miracle
Walking without a Brace and other blessings

"And Jesus went about all Galilee, teaching in their synagogues, and preaching the gospel of the kingdom, and healing all manner of sickness and all manner of disease among the people."

Matt. 4:23

*G*od answered another prayer. After several years of having to walk with a brace on my left leg or walk with crutches, God gave me another miracle. He healed my left leg and enabled me to walk without using crutches or having to continue to wear the brace. Several people were in our prayer group and were praying for healing for me specifically in my leg. One morning I woke up and somehow felt different. I usually reached for my crutch to use to help me walk to the bathroom. That morning, I didn't reach for the crutch, but I stood up and took a step and my leg didn't give way. I continued to walk to the bathroom without the aid of the crutch or my brace. I was so excited. Jerry had already left for work, and we didn't have cell phones back then so I had to wait until I was sure he was in his office to call him and tell him I had walked to the bathroom and back to the bedroom without my crutch or brace. When I was able to reach him, I told him what I had done and in his quiet manner, he said,

"Well, isn't that what we have been praying for. Does it surprise you that God has answered our prayers and healed your leg? I've been expecting it. Have a good day. I have to go now."

As I thought about his quiet manner and acceptance that God was going to answer our prayers, I felt ashamed at my lack of faith and I immediately thanked God for my healing and that I would seek His will for my life without hesitation and doubt. I also thanked Him for my very special husband who accepted Christ several years after I did, but had a gift of childlike faith and trust that apparently I did not have and I needed to work on my growing in Christ as my husband was growing faster than I was and I needed to learn from him how to pray believing that God was going to answer my prayer and realize that God was not on my time table, but He was always with me and knew what I needed and when I needed it.

Our daughter had married and moved to Belgium with her husband who was in the Army and in June 1974 we were blessed with our first grandchild. Jerry, Steven and I flew to Belgium to greet our new grandson, James Edward. He was such a precious gift from God. He was so tiny and all arms and legs. Even now, writing this down, I think back to the first time I held him in my arms and offered a prayer of thanksgiving that he was normal and healthy. As he grew, it was apparent that God had blessed him with the gift of music, writing, singing, playing different instruments.

While we were in Belgium, Buzzy served as a camp counselor at a youth retreat in Greenville. One evening they went into town. The camp director was in one car with two other teens and Buzzy was in his car with two other teens. They were returning back to the camp when a car drove out of a driveway and Buzzy's car crashed into his. The young man driving the other car was admittedly on drugs. He was being chased with a shotgun by the man who lived in the house. He also had two other youth in his car. Fortunately, no one was seriously injured. The camp director witnessed the accident. The young man who was driving the other car was 21, no job, no income, no home, no driver's license, no tags on the car and no insurance. We were grateful that no one was seriously injured. When we returned from Belgium we were met with the news that Buzzy's car was totaled and so was the other car. No charges were filed against anyone. We filed the report with our insurance company and when I went to pick up the check I asked what would happen to the young man that caused the accident. The agent told me that the driver of the other car would have to pay the insurance company back before he could get a driver's license. I asked if that was all the punishment he would receive. The agent told me that I seemed vindictive and wanted him to be severely punished. I said that I wasn't, but I wanted him to understand that his careless act could have caused six young people to be killed or seriously hurt. I still do not understand why our laws work so hard to protect the guilty and do nothing to help or protect the victims. We could have filed a law suit against the young man, but it would have cost us $600 and it still would not have made the young man aware of what he did. We were thankful that no one was seriously injured. A car can be replaced, but a life can't.

Seven years later on December 23, 1980, our second grandchild was born. We felt so blessed that this baby was normal and healthy. Our son Jerry Jr. was so proud of his son Jerry James. J. J. has a strong faith today and has provided us with 5 great-grandchildren.

In December 1987, our youngest son, Steven Michael presented us with our third grandchild (our only granddaughter), Ashley Lauren. We felt we had been blessed again with a granddaughter who was perfect in every way. As Ashley grew she participated in the creative ministries program and it was evident to see that God had blessed her with natural creative abilities working with puppets, interpretive movement as well as playing the piano and singing.

J. J., Ashley, James

We felt it a little strange that our three grandchildren were 7 years apart. James (Jimmy) was 7 when Jerry James (J.J.) was born and James was 14, Jerry James 7 when Ashley was born. Our Steven was 10 when Jimmy was born. Jimmy said Steven picked on him while growing up. When Jerry James (J.J.) was born he said that Jimmy picked on him. When Steven announced they were expecting and didn't know it was a girl or boy, J. J. said he hoped it was a boy so he could pick on him the way Jimmy had picked on him. When Ashley was born, J. J. said he was disappointed because you just couldn't pick on a girl and he felt cheated. We just felt very blessed to have our precious grandchildren in our lives.

As I write this book, I want to say how blessed we are to have a new grandson. Our son, Steven, said he felt blessed to have a daughter, Ashley, who will be 25 on Dec. 28, 2012 and a son, Michael Thomas, who will be 3 on Dec. 19, 2012. Michael was actually born on my sister's birthday, December 19. She has her own son, Ricky, who was born on her birthday and now she has a great-nephew who will celebrate her birthday as it is now his birthday, too. We can't wait to see what God has in store for this newest member of our family.

Michael

It would not be appropriate for me to leave our family as stated above because due to circumstances, we have added several step grandchildren and step great-grandchildren and one step great-great grandson to our family. We thank God for blessing us and extending our family. One of our precious step-grandson's, Richard, was killed three years ago in an automobile accident. We miss him, but we know he is with the Lord and will be waiting for us when God calls us home.

Jerry often wrote me notes wishing me a good day and telling me he loved me. He would leave them on the refrigerator (he knew I went there often). For our 32nd wedding anniversary he wrote me the following poem, had his secretary type it up and put it in a frame. On August 31st, 1984 he gave me the poem and a dozen yellow roses. I have included a copy of the poem just as he wrote and signed it. He had such a quiet, special way of always letting me know how much he loved me. I sincerely hope that everyone, at some point in their lives, will experience the special kind of love we shared that can only come from God.

In 1986 I was working on my Master's Degree, teaching school, and serving as music and youth director at Capital View Baptist Church. One of the classes I took was a creative writing class and in this class the instructor wanted us to take something from our past and if there was someone we needed to thank for something special they had done during that time to construct a letter to them as part of our creative writing project. I chose to write a thank you letter to my mother. Instead of my telling you what I wrote I will share the letter with you.

THIRTY-TWO YEARS AGO

Thirty-two years ago I decided to take a wife,
one I could live with the rest of my life.

Thirty-two years ago when we first got started,
it wasn't long before we were parted.

Thirty-two years ago seems like a long time,
but when two people love each other it's short and sublime.

Thirty-two years ago we didn't know what direction to go,
because we had no one to ask all the time "Is this so."

In thirty-two years there has been plenty of ups and downs,
but at the end of the day there are always sweet sounds.

Thirty-two years ago we embarked on something new,
and still today when we're together we're never blue.

Thirty-two years ago we took our solemn vows;
after all this passed time we are still pals.

Thirty two years ago we were both very young;
after all these years our song is still being sung.

Thirty-two years ago we were blessed with each other,
after all this time together we still love one another.

Thirty-two years ago and three children later,
if it were to do over I'd still mate her.

Thirty-two years ago we started something sweet,
today after thirty-two years it's a real treat.

After all of this you have no card,
Because on this I worked too hard.

Dear Mother,

I wonder if you know just how special you are to me. I have tried to thank you in many ways for all the things you have done for me. Somehow, when I review all those things my thanks seem very small. Something wonderful happened to me recently and it made me realize just how really special you are. I want to share that something with you.

On April 10, 1986 I was selected as Caughman Road Middle School's Teacher of the year. The award is significant within itself. However, as you will know right away, it is doubly important to me since it was given on April 10th. I'm sure you remember another April 10th - the year is 1954. I won't bring back all the memories I know you have concerning that day, but I want to thank you for your faith and belief that God would let me live and that the phone call made to you telling you I had been killed in an automobile accident was wrong. Mother, your love is next to God's love. It has to be. I don't know any other way to measure the love you shared by staying with me twenty-four hours a day seven days a week for three weeks. You did everything for me and asked nothing in return. Even after those three weeks, it took several months of care before I was able to care for myself. During all that time you never complained. You passed your strength on to me and gave me a deep faith that I could do anything if I set my mind to it and asked God to help.

Well, Mother, after your encouragement, guidance and assistance I did get better and I became a teacher. I wanted to share with others the things you had taught me as well as things I had learned through study and experience. I prayed often that I would be effective in my teaching just as you had been effective in yours and on April 10, 1986, my peers gave me the highest recognition they could give. I know that you share my joy just as you have shared my pain. I also know that you will feel as I do, that God is somehow saying, "You have used your life to help others."

Mother, my friend, my confidant, my inspiration, I humbly say, Thank You from the bottom of my heart and I love you dearly. You are my Teacher of the Year

Love,

My instructor at USC wrote this on the bottom of my paper:

"Heartfelt and moving. Are you or can you send it to her? What a tribute!"

During this same class, we were asked to select something from our past that was significant in changing our lives. Of course it was easy for me since although I was born on September 18, 1935, I have a new birthday, April 10, 1954. I was born again as a Christian at the age of 13 when I accepted Christ as my Savior, but I believe God gave me new life (or extended my life) after being pronounced Dead on Arrival at McLeod Infirmary in Florence, SC when I met him during my out of body experience and I asked him to give me enough time to lead my husband to the Lord as I didn't want to be separated from him for all eternity. In those early hours on April 10th, God felt and heard my plea and granted my request. I now believe that April 10th began a new life for me. Naturally, I chose to write about the accident that changed my life forever. To make it a little harder, we had to write three drafts in poetry format, with each draft reducing the number of words used to describe the event. I am including the three drafts and inserting the professor's comments at the end.

Draft #1　　　　　　April 10 – A Special Day in My Life

Happy and secure was I
There was no reason to cry
I had things that money couldn't buy
There was no thought that I might die

Driving overnight so we could spend
A precious few nights with our kin
The right of way, my husband tried to lend
Because he knew that metal wouldn't bend

It didn't matter, the other driver was asleep
Even blowing the horn, from him brought no peep
The two cars came together in a great heap
Crushing metal was a sound our memory would keep

In the emergency room, two hours had passed
The doctor said, "It's too late, her time didn't last
But great are the powers that God has
His strength He gave me in great mass

The day was April 10, 1954
From all the bruises I was really sore
But staying in bed was a real bore

Twelve Miracles Including a Glimpse of Heaven

The accident had opened up a new door

32 years ago He granted me my life
He didn't promise it would be free from strife
He did allow me to remain Jerry's wife
For that I'm so grateful I could play the fife

The speaker blared through the air
From the children, there wasn't a snear
And at me, they all began to stare
Their smiles revealed their deep care

Mrs. Hartsoe is our Teacher of the Year
The children burst out with a cheer
My joy was one I could hardly bare
April 10, 1954 and April 10, 1986, what a pair

It makes me wonder and sometimes I cry
It's hard to believe, no matter how hard I try
So I just accept my fate and give a big sigh
Because I'm happy that on April 10, 1954, I didn't have to die.

Draft #2   April 10th

Crashing metal
Breaking glass
Twisted bodies
Unfelt pain
Life and death
April 10, 1954

Flashing lights
Clean white sheets
Hovering people
Shaking heads
Darkness
April 10, 1954

Weightless floating
Downward view
Looking up
Colors and music
Indescribable
April 10, 1954

Realization

White Sheet Removed

Bright lights

Sterile room

Life – a thin thread

April 10, 1954

Broken bones

Torn tissue

Bruises abound

No pain

Sightless eyes

April 10, 1954

Sight partially restored

Bones mended

Exercise

Great effort

Time passes

And heals

Another year

Children

School

Work

Time passes

And heals

Years later

Thirty-two

Exactly

Reward

Teacher of the Year

April 10, 1986

Two days

Same date

Different years

Fate intervenes

April 10, 1954 and 1986

Twelve Miracles Including a Glimpse of Heaven

Draft #3   April 10th

    Bending metal

    Crashing glass

    Broken body

    <u>No life</u>

    <u>Wait</u>

    <u>Maybe</u>

    <u>Yes</u>

    <u>Breath returns</u>

    Life restored

    Pain

    Mending

    Extended life

    Useful

    Productive

    Award

    Teacher of the Year

    Two acts

    Same day

    Connected

    Years apart

    April 10, 1954

    April 10, 1986

Instructor's comments: Seems very clear, powerful. I was totally involved, emotionally living it with you – especially nerve tingling is the section I underlined.

Question I asked the Instructor: In the third draft – did I include enough information or was it detailed enough to explain what I was talking about?

Instructor's answer: Yes, yes! It was so powerful. I had tears in my eyes all over again. At no point did I feel led into irrelevancies. I could follow the movements and your feelings clearly.

Chapter Ten

The Ninth Miracle - Creative Ministries

""Make a joyful noise unto the Lord, all the earth: make a loud noise, and rejoice, and sing praise. Sing unto the Lord with the harp; with the harp, and the voice of a psalm. With trumpets and sound of cornet make a joyful noise before the Lord, the King; ... Let the floods clap their hands; let the hills be joyful together . . ."

Psalm 98: 4-6; 8

*I*n 1993 I was music director at Southside Baptist Church and it was a transition time in the music life of churches. Creative ministries had started in several churches using contemporary Christian music and interpretive movement along with dramatic skits and, yes, even clowning. This interested me very much. It also interested several of the choir members and we formed a creative ministries group. We attended workshops, wrote skits, and the choir presented the first cantata with (as some of the older choir members called it) canned music (orchestrated music on tape).

We began to get requests to go to other churches and present creative ministry programs. One of our choir members, Norma, had just retired from the telephone company and she took a class in making puppets and she made several puppets for us to use. She was so talented and made black light puppets which are so special to use. It was an exciting time and we were invited to help other churches form their own creative ministries. We were able, with the help of the church, to purchase a closed in trailer to carry our puppets, stage, lighting, etc. in as we traveled to other locations.

Popcorn (Jerry) and Chatter (Nellie)

Iceman (Buzzy) and Snowflake (Cindy)

During this time my nephew and niece, Ricky and Cathi, began working with us and I am happy to say that they are still doing creative ministries as I am writing this in 2012. I had to stop several years ago because my hands would not work well enough to move the puppets mouths, and due to leg instability I could not stoop and stand long enough to do a program. When we are unable to do something God has enabled us to do, He always has someone else prepared to continue the task. What a great God we serve. The years of active creative ministry were some of the most enjoyable and fulfilling times in my entire life. To be able to use the creative abilities to share God's love and the message of salvation to others was a blessing and I believe it was a gift from God and was a miracle given to me during a transition time. If I had not had to slow down and wait on the Lord I might have missed one of the greatest blessings in my life. I know that some people feel that creative ministries should not be presented in church, but if you read your Bible you will find that Jesus used creative methods to bring His message to the multitude. He preached in the synagogue, in a boat, on the riverside, on top of a mountain, in a garden, in the upper room, beside a water well and as He walked along the road. He used storytelling, parables, and examples to present His message. He preached and taught everyone who would listen and many were born again and received the gift of salvation and the promise of eternal life. We witnessed many who accepted Jesus as their Savior during the creative ministries programs. Cathi recently told me that at one of their creative ministry puppet programs several children accepted Christ as their Savior and it was a wonderful time of rejoicing.

Creative Ministries Troupe

Chapter Eleven

The Tenth Miracle - Life without Jerry

"That whosoever believeth in him should not perish, but have eternal life."

John 3:15

"Peace I leave with you, my peace I give unto you: not as the world giveth, give I unto you. Let not your heart be troubled, neither let it be afraid."

John 14:27

I retired from teaching public school in 1988. I had taken a position at a Technical College as Curriculum Coordinator and I also bought a Florist Shop. This was a really unusual experience. My son-in-law's father had died and I went into the florist shop to select flowers to send to the funeral home and the lady asked me if I would be interested in buying her shop. I had never been creative with materials. I was creative with words, but not with flowers. I talked it over with my mother who was one of the most creative people I have ever known. She could take a little nothing and make something beautiful out of it. She knew I did not inherit that trait from her, but she told me that I was a teacher so I could teach myself and if I was determined enough I could do it.

I also discussed it with Jerry and he said it was up to me. That summer we bought a new van and took our three grandsons (Jimmy, Joe, and J.J.) on a vacation trip across the country. We covered 18 states and were gone a month. When we came back I discussed the details with the owner and bought the shop. She left it well stocked with live and artificial arrangements. She had also agreed to work with me the first month and teach me how to make arrangements. Within the first two days I had sold almost everything out of the cooler (fresh flowers) and several artificial arrangements. The lady did not show up. After the third day I called her and asked her if she was coming in to show me how to make arrangements as I needed to fill the cooler and I had several orders for delivery. She said she was not going to come, but she could recommend someone for me to hire that could make arrangements. I did not have a choice and so after three days I realized I may have made a mistake and dealt with someone who did not intend to keep her part of the contract. I hired the person she recommended. It was very scary because I didn't know if I would make enough money to pay rent, utilities, buy more flowers, and pay an employee.

We made it through with God's help and before I knew it six months had gone by and it was time for Valentine's Day. I have the greatest respect for florists at Valentine's Day and Mother's Day, the two busiest times of the year for florists. I must tell you how I learned to make casket sprays. My sister came to my rescue. She did inherit the creative talent from our mother and she came in after she got off work and helped me make arrangements. The first time someone came in and ordered a casket spray they picked it out of the book. My sister and I went to the cemetery and very reverently looked at the casket sprays and flower baskets and other arrangements on new graves to see how to create the arrangements. The reason they came to us to order the flowers was that they were from out of town and it was Saturday and not many other shops were open and they needed it early the next morning as the funeral was to be Sunday afternoon since they had to leave town on Monday. This would be the last thing they could do for their loved ones and wanted it to be very special. I must say the arrangements we made turned out really pretty and the customer was very pleased.

Shortly after buying the shop and realizing that the previous owner had no intention of honoring her commitment to teach me, I had tried to find a class to go to or a correspondence course to help me learn, but none were available. Thanks to the natural abilities of my sister, niece, and oldest son we did very well. We soon became engrossed with weddings, funerals, birthdays, holidays and after a year I opened a small shop at the University of South Carolina, but we closed it six months later because everything shut down in the summer in the area we were located at the university and there was no income to keep it going. They did not provide us with parking or delivery space so we decided it was best to close it.

The first shop I bought had a small stream behind it and several months after I bought the shop we were working in the work room getting ready for a big wedding (it was also Mother's Day weekend) and my sister, my niece, my son, and Essie (the lady I hired to help) and I were really busy. All of a sudden my niece yelled "Snake". We looked where she was pointing and there was very large snake getting ready to come across the room to the table where we were working. All of us ran into the showroom. There were several customers in the shop and my son said,

"Oh, my goodness, why are you'll afraid of a little snake."

By that time the snake had reached the table and curled up under one end of the table. My son picked up the broom and placed it on top of the snake and the snake started uncoiling and it was about five feet long. My son took the broom away and came into the show room and said,

"Maybe we need to call the animal people."

That's what we did. We carefully moved everything we were working on into the show room because we had to finish the flowers for the wedding and time was running out. The customer's were curious and just hung around waiting on the animal catchers. They came and caught the snake and said it wasn't poisonous. It was a rat snake. They said we didn't have to worry about rats. We didn't think that was funny, but they did.

The Tenth Miracle - Life without Jerry

Several days later, one afternoon we were working in the work room. A customer came in and wanted to know if we had any Mother's Day cards left. My niece went to the shelf in the work room to get them and when she moved a box several small snakes began to crawl out. We again called the animal people and they said the snake they had taken away was a female and these were the babies. They then checked in the ceiling and the bathroom and found several more snakes. I quickly called the landlord and gave him notice that we would be moving across the street. We could not work in a building that had snakes. So thirty days later we relocated the shop across the street.

We felt like God had kept us safe because we had spent many nights in that work room making flowers and did not know that we had company. I kept the shop for two years and then I sold it. The work in the florist shop was the most exhausting work I have ever had to do, but the rewards were wonderful. We were able to see the beauty in the many different kinds of flowers and greenery that God had created. To see someone smile at the beautiful arrangements and know it was going to brighten someone's day was the best reward. To finish the flowers for a wedding and know that they would be used to help celebrate the beginning of two people becoming one always brought a smile to our faces knowing we had a small part in that joyous occasion. The most rewarding was when we made funeral flowers. Knowing that this was the last thing we could do to help the loved ones of the deceased deal with the loss brought us the most joy.

Since I could not find a class to teach me how to make arrangements, after I learned how and bought books and read and studied about flowers, I, with the help of my brother, Gene, created three floral videos showing how to make wedding flowers, live arrangements, and artificial arrangements. I did learn how to create beautiful arrangements, but my sister, my niece, and my son inherited mother's gift of creativity and their arrangements seemed to have something special in them that mine did not. My arrangements were done mechanically because it was the right way to do it, but their arrangements had something special about them.

I sold the shop because I needed to go back to teaching full time in order to give us a set income. In 1988, Jerry began having seizures that would freeze his body. In other words he would cease to have any movement, but he was unaware that he couldn't move. They would only last a few minutes, but could be dangerous. One evening we were on our way home and he was driving and I realized that the car was pulling to the right of the road. I called his name and he didn't respond. I grabbed the steering wheel and tried to turn it back to the road, but his grip was frozen and we were headed off the road. I gave a pull with all my strength and it turned us back to the road and he asked me what I was doing and I told him he had apparently blacked out and we were heading off the road. He said that it had happened a couple of times before, but he caught himself before hitting anything.

We decided it was time for him to go to the doctor to see what was wrong. We knew he had grand mal seizures, but he always had a warning (a tingle in his left arm) and could stop whatever he was doing before the seizure and they were adequately controlled by medicine. In fact, they had determined that it was safe for him to drive. In February, 1989 he went into the VA hospital for tests. It was determined that he was now having three different kinds of seizures and would not be able to drive anymore. He was changed from the 70% disabled when he retired from the service to 100% permanently disabled. He was 56 years old. Of course he had to resign his job because it required him to drive. I really believe he was relieved because he had felt unsure of himself for some time, but was reluctant to say anything about it. It took seven months to get his salary adjustments and social security started. It was obvious that I needed to return to teaching to provide us with a steady income.

The school district asked me to establish a program that would teach girls job skills. These particular girls were teens that had gotten pregnant, dropped out of school and were on welfare. The district wanted to help them prepare for work so they could complete their high school requirements to graduate and be able to get a job that didn't require college so they would be able to be removed from the welfare rolls. The school would also provide child care while they were in classes and the child care section would also serve as training for those who wanted to work in child care facilities.

I developed a program that included learning to use word processing, data entry and Business English. It proved to be very successful. In fact, I was selected Teacher of the Year for Atlas Road

Learning Center, which was part of Richland School District One. I did that for two years and then the funding was cut and the program was closed.

Jerry was enjoying his retirement. He did just what he wanted to do, when he wanted to do it. He was very forgetful and would turn the water on and forget to turn it off and sometimes it would run for hours. We were told that the medicine he had been taking since 1957 was destroying his brain cells and his only choice to stop the deteriation was to stop taking the medicine and if he chose to stop taking the medicine they could not guarantee that he would not have multiple seizures daily. He made the decision to continue taking the medicine because he said he would rather have his brain die than to deal with the seizures.

Jerry was afraid to go out of the house because he was scared he would get lost and not know how to find his way back home. It was also a difficult financial time for us. We decided to sell our house and move to an apartment where there would be other people around to help keep check on him while I was in school. We found an apartment close to a shopping area.

During the time we lived in the apartment, Jerry's mother had to have heart surgery and she never fully recovered from it. She lived a year after the surgery and was in the hospital thirteen times during that year. Sometimes when she was not in the hospital she stayed with us. Jerry was the only child she had and she could not accept that he had some medical problems that prevented him from living a full, active life at that time. It was hard on him having to take care of her when he could barely take care of himself. She begged not to go to a nursing home so I accepted a position to do a drama program at a juvenile facility to see if it would help with rehabilitation of young people who had committed a multitude of crimes and were serving time to pay for them. While incarcerated they went to school to earn high school credits so they could receive a high school diploma. I did this for two years. I wrote grants both years and received $20,000 each year to bring in different forms of art and artists to the students.

I could write a book about those two years. It was a blessing to me and I hope it was to the students who were involved in the program. It was also frustrating due to the lack of care being provided to the inmates. Over the two years I had a total of 200 students, 15 at a time. When someone was paroled, I held auditions and selected a student to fill the vacancy. We wrote plays, produced them, created a magazine, and printed copies for everyone in the school. I had students who were convicted of rape, murder, armed robbery, and running away from home. Statistics indicated that every month 60 – 75 students were released on probation and within three months 75% of those released had broken probation or committed another crime and were returned to jail. In the two years and 200 students in the drama program (all had been released when I decided I needed to be home with Jerry) only 5 had to return. During the time there, I had the privilege of leading 16 young people to accept the Lord as their Savior. What a joy that was. It simply proves that when you treat people with respect and help them realize that they have potential to succeed, that they will do just that. Even today, some of the students still keep in contact with me.

One of the reasons I did this program was to help care for Jerry's mother. The hospital found me homes with registered nurses that would care for her in their home twenty-four hours a day and it would be better than in a nursing home. The cost was $2,000 a month. That was my salary, but I was glad I could do it because it was too hard on Jerry for her to be at our house. He was having a difficult time dealing with his own problems which were getting worse.

While serving as music director at Southside we became good friends with one of the members, Dorcas Corley. Her husband had died and she began to travel with us. In 1998 we took our second cross-country trip. Since Jerry couldn't drive, I drove. Jerry and Dorcas tried to read the maps and keep us on track, but most of the time I was reading the map, driving, and trying to find our way. We were gone a month and visited many of the places we had visited 10 years earlier when we took the trip with our three grandsons. Dorcas had not travelled very much and it was wonderful sharing some of the things we had done in 1988 and also doing some new things and visiting new places. It became a joke that I had told Dorcas that if I died first, I was willing Jerry to her because I knew they would look after each other. Sadly, she was left with me instead of Jerry. That part of the story will come a little later in the book.

After our trip in the summer of 1998 Jerry began having difficulty walking, sitting, standing, etc. The neurologist told him that the nerves in his legs were almost dead and this was why he was having so much pain. As with so many things, there wasn't anything that could be done to prevent the nerves from dying. It was also suspected that he may have cancer. We made appointments at the VA and they kept being postponed, put off, delayed and all the time he was getting worse.

In December 1999, our daughter and her husband decided they wanted to move further out into the country and buy a house that had some land with it. Both my son and daughter had settled in the Lexington area. They had been asking us to move on the Lexington side of town so they would be closer to help with their daddy. So, when my daughter and her husband decided to move I asked what they planned to do with their house. My daughter said that they would either sell it or rent it. I told her that we would buy their house. In December 1999 they moved and we moved.

In January 2000, the English Department Chairperson from a local Technical College asked me to teach an English class. I agreed, but instead of teaching one class I taught 2 classes. Almost 12 years later as I am trying to finish this

50TH Anniversary

book, I am still teaching at the College. Since I do not want to teach full time I only teach two days a week and usually teach 2 - 4 classes.

On August 31, 2002, Jerry and I celebrated fifty years of marriage. We talked a lot about how blessed we were and we reflected on the accident and how it had changed our lives. It felt a little strange that we remembered the wreck, that both cars were totaled, that the young man's father took him out of the hospital without being discharged and that he had been charged $17 for driving to the left of the center line, but never paid the fine. Neither one of us knew the young man's name and as I write this book I do not know what happened to him. We were told that he had a broken kneecap and two teeth knocked out. He was twenty-one, just discharged from the Navy, had partied that evening and started on his way to his home in Ohio and fell asleep at the wheel.

When we looked back over 50 years we realized again how blessed we were. I had asked God for enough time to lead my husband to salvation and He had granted that wish and given us 48 years since that time. We talked about growing in Christ and felt we had tried, but had not always sought His Will and we asked God to forgive us for not always trusting Him and we thanked and praised His Name for all His goodness. Our children gave us a beautiful party and we shared our day with lots of family and friends. We returned to Charleston and revisited the home where we were married. It is painted pink now, but the people who live there were nice enough to allow us to go inside. They told us that the previous owners had taken out or closed up the fireplace, but when they bought the house they put it back in – so, there we were looking at the same stairs I had walked down holding onto my father's arm and the same French glass doors that I had breezed through (remembering Scarlet O'Hara) and the fireplace (a little different bricks) where I stood and joined my life with a special young man with the most beautiful, big, brown eyes that I had ever seen, fifty years ago.

After moving to our present home in West Columbia, we began attending Kitti Wake Baptist Church. Soon after we began attending the church welcomed a new pastor and his family. Prior to our move, I had served as music director at Southside Baptist Church for 10 years. When I resigned, they asked my daughter to take the position. She has been there over 10 years. When the pastor at Kitti Wake found out that I had been music director at Southside he asked me to meet with the committee to see about leading the music at Kitti Wake. I accepted to be interim music director and asked the committee to continue looking for a permanent music director. I was beginning to have difficulty standing for long periods of time. Jerry was getting worse and needed me more at home. I knew I needed more time with Jerry so I, along with many others, began praying for God to bring someone to lead the music. I had told the committee that I needed to have the time with Jerry. They also offered to pay me for directing the music. God had blessed us and we did not need the money at that time and this was a gift of talent that God had blessed me with and I had used it for 50 years so I did not accept pay, but I told them that this was a way I could serve the Lord and return the gift that He had given to me many years before.

During the time I served as music director we did a dinner theatre Christmas play "The Read Meaning of Christmas" that I wrote and directed. In my previous church I had written and directed an Easter Cantata entitled "A Promise Fulfilled" and recently one of the members whom I did not know had seen the cantata when we did it at Southside, asked me why we couldn't do it at Kitti Wake. I told her that that was up to God if we decided to do it or not. Many who saw it (we actually have presented it several times) said that I should send it in to a music company for publication. Perhaps that will be the next task God leads me to do - Write for publication some of the children's stories, plays, and poetry I have written through the years.

God is so good and He always provides our needs. He sent James Jacobs to the church. James had led music at Red Bank Baptist church and then moved out of town and had just returned to Columbia in May, 2004. He was hired and was to begin the first Sunday in June. The timing was perfect.

I had become tired of waiting on the VA to schedule an appointment with the oncologist, so, I made an appointment with a civilian oncologist. After examining Jerry and running some tests he said he felt that Jerry had some suspicious areas and needed to have a special bone x-ray scan. Jerry was scheduled to have a bone biopsy on Friday, July 2. On Thursday, July 1, he had to go to the VA and have a special bone scan x-ray series run. We went to the VA that morning and he had the x-rays taken and was scheduled to see the oncologist that afternoon. After the x-rays we went to the snack bar to have lunch. We met a friend Jerry had served with and sat with him and his wife. Jerry liked Whopper Hamburgers, but it had been months since he had been able to eat more than half of a burger. I ordered him a Whopper, fries and a Pepsi. While we were talking with our friends, Jerry tapped me on the shoulder and pointed to his plate. He had eaten the entire Whopper and part of the fries. He was so pleased with himself. As it turned out, that was the last solid food he would be able to eat – his last meal.

We went to see the oncologist and Jerry told her that he was scheduled to have the bone biopsy the next day. She told him that he could not see an outside doctor and continue coming to the VA. That upset me. I didn't like the VA or trust them because of prior incidents, but Jerry was military through and through and he trusted them. He told her he was going to have the bone biopsy with the civilian doctor. He told her he liked him and trusted him. He told her after the report from the bone biopsy he would make up his mind what to do.

We left the hospital and he, using his walker, walked to the car although I offered to go get the car and pick him up. He said he felt like walking so we walked the short distance to the car. On the way home we stopped by the Hot Dog place on Rosewood Dr. He wanted a strawberry milkshake. I stopped and started to get out to get our shakes and he stopped me and said he would go get them. I said o.k. He got out and walked the few steps to the window to order the shakes. I noticed that he was leaning on the little ledge at the window and I started to get out to go help him and the girl handed him the shakes. He walked over to my window and handed me the milkshakes. He held on to the front of the car and walked around and got in the passenger's seat and took his milkshake. I backed out and started home. I asked him if what the VA doctor had said upset him about choosing which doctor to go to. He said no, it had not upset him. He then looked over at me and said, "Do you think we can feel a little bit angry at the guy that hit us."

I replied, "I don't think it would change anything."

I looked over at him and saw his hand was shaking very badly. I asked him if he was o.k. and I reached over and took the milkshake out of his hand and put it in the cup holder. He said in a very slurred speech,

"I'm just like you, I gotta go to sleep." And with that he slumped over. We were closer home than the hospital, but I knew this wasn't a seizure, it was something else.

I drove home and called the office for my son or my son-in-law and told the receptionist that I needed one of them at home as quick as they could get there. In just a few minutes Tom came and I was trying to get Jerry to a sitting position, not slumped over like he was and Tom thought I was trying to get him out of the car. I told Tom I was trying to straighten him up and I believed he had a stroke. Tom quickly got in the driver's seat and I got in the back seat and we went to Lexington County Hospital.

Someone met us at the car with a wheelchair, but he quickly realized that Jerry could not sit in a wheelchair so they brought a gurney to the car and two people lifted him out of the car and onto the gurney and rushed him in the emergency room. They quickly determined that he had suffered a stroke. They debated on whether to give him the shot to prevent further damage, but it was decided that with the other medication he was on it would be too dangerous to give him the shot. They were going to admit him to the hospital, but they had to wait on a room. By this time Jerry had regained consciousness. The nurse started pulling his shirt off over his head and with his dry sense of humor and slurred speech he said, "Be careful and don't mess my hair up." Everyone laughed. They needed to move him to another room in the emergency room area to wait on a room in the hospital. They removed all the machines and left him in a small room. He needed to urinate, but couldn't so they inserted a catheter. Several hours had past and they brought a tray with liquids for him to eat, but he was unable to swallow. Terri asked them why they had removed all the machines and why he was not being monitored. The nurse said it wasn't necessary as he had had several of these episodes and he would probably be fine in the morning. She quickly informed them that he had never had an "episode" like that before and until 3 p.m. that afternoon he had been fine and could do everything for himself without help. The nurse quickly brought back the equipment and hooked him back up so he could be monitored.

The next morning they had put him in a room. His left side would not move the night before but he was moving his left arm a little bit. The nurse was giving him a neurological examination and was at the foot of the bed and had run a tool over the bottom of his foot. Buzzy was on the right side of the bed and I was on the left side of the bed. Suddenly Buzzy looked at me and I looked at him and I said,

"Your daddy has just had another stroke!" Buzzy said,

"I know, Mom, I felt it go from his head to his feet." After that he never moved his left side again. They did another brain scan and said he had a massive stroke and should be dead. The first stroke the day before had left swelling in his brain and they were giving him medicine to reduce the swelling in his brain. Jerry continued to recognize us and could talk a little, but could not swallow so he had to be suctioned out and his medication and food had to be fed to him intravenously. They said if they couldn't get the swelling in his brain to stop and reduce that he could not live more than 72 hours. He held on seven days. He knew us; we had time to make final decisions. He knew he was going to die. He was ready to meet Jesus. He kept his sense of humor and tried to cheer us up. He talked with Pastor Tim and told him he was ready to meet Jesus and his family.

When we were married my father told Jerry that he felt sorry for him and Jerry asked him why. Daddy told Jerry that he was getting the radio but they forgot to include the knob to turn me off. We joked and I told him that he better not tell daddy he was right about the radio. We also joked about the fact that I was the Elvis fan and he was going to see him in heaven before I did. I told him to tell Elvis

I still listened to his music and Jerry had taped his movies for me.

Lots of people were praying and visiting Jerry in the hospital. I was teaching a summer school class in the mornings so Buzzy stayed with his daddy while I was in class and then I went to the hospital for the afternoon. Terri came when she got off from work and gave me a break to go home, shower and come back to spend the night. Jerry knew he couldn't swallow, but he wanted to try one more time to see if he could swallow. They had talked about putting in a feeding tube in his side, but before he would agree to do that he wanted to try one more time. They felt it was unnecessary, but I insisted they honor his request and try one last time. They tried on that Thursday afternoon and they tried three different times, but he was unable to swallow.

On that Thursday evening, a week after the stroke three male friends came to visit him and each one had served in a different branch of the military and they had a wonderful conversation arguing about which branch of the military was the best. Of course, each one felt that their branch was the best. That night was the last night that Jerry was conscious enough to talk.

On Friday, he was in great distress trying to breathe so they put an oxygen bag over his nose and mouth. The doctor recommended that they put him on a morphine drip to make him more comfortable as they had not been able to stop the swelling in his brain and he had very little time left. I asked them not to stop his medicine because I didn't want him to have to deal with a seizure. The doctor told me they had not stopped his seizure medicine but that he had had several seizures during the past week. I told the doctor that I didn't want him to starve to death. The doctor said he would not starve to death because he would not live long enough to starve to death. In fact, the doctor continued, we are amazed that he is still alive. The second stroke he had was massive and he should not have survived it. I guess he had some unfinished business and that's what has kept him alive and conscious.

As I said before, Jerry never lost his sense of humor. After he retired he assumed the duties of washing clothes and dishes. Somehow he had forgotten that out of the 18 years we were married with him on active duty with the Army that we were separated 9 of those years when he was stationed somewhere that we could not go with him. However, that was his choice to do and he (even if we had guests) would always load the dishwasher. On one of our conversations during those precious days, I told him he needed to fight to stay with me because after all he had said I didn't know how to wash clothes or load the dishwasher. He replied,

"I'm a man, I managed. You're a woman so you can womanage." Now when I wash clothes or dishes, I tell him that I am womanaging.

Dorcas had come to sit with us on Friday evening and when she was leaving I told her I would love to have a hot donut and she said she would pick some up early in the morning and come sit with us on Saturday. That Friday night I didn't rest well because Jerry was not conscious and his breathing was so shallow. When I took my spit bath in the morning I left the bathroom door open a little so I could see him. Dorcas got there around 8 a.m. with hot donuts. I ate a donut and the phone rang. It was my sister calling to check on Jerry. I told her he was not breathing strong, but there had been little change from the day before. I hung up and walked around the bed and picked up a donut and sat down and started to take a bite when I noticed that Jerry was not breathing. I told Dorcas that he wasn't breathing and I put the donut down, got up, walked to the bed, put my hand on his arm and shook him and said, "Breathe, Jerry, Breathe!" He never opened his eyes, but he took one deep breath and then stopped breathing for good. I shook him again, but there was no response. I pushed the button and told the nurse that he was not breathing. I picked up the phone and called the children. I went to the door and looked down to the nurse's station and called and said " Mr. Hartsoe is not breathing!" Then I realized that no one was coming. Jerry had a living will that said do not resuscitate and I knew he was gone. It was time. God had been so gracious to us to give us a week to say goodbye. Dorcas asked if she could kiss him goodbye and I told her she could. The children got there very quickly. Everyone was on alert expecting it at anytime. Our youngest son had come the week end before and went back to St. Louis and then was on his way back to Columbia. He didn't get to the hospital in time to say goodbye, but he had said his goodbyes the weekend before just in case he didn't make it back in time.

It was so hard to walk out of that hospital room and leave my dear husband of almost 52 years behind, but I knew he wasn't in that room or that body anymore. He was safe in the arms of Jesus and having a joyous reunion with all of his family. His mother was the 11th child of 12 and the last to die. Jerry lived with his grandmother until he was 13 and she died. Now he would be reunited with both of them.

As I looked back on those last few moments in that hospital room I believe that Jerry knew the angels were there for him and that final deep breath he took was his goodbye to me.

I believe that God knows the purpose He has for our lives and when we are connected to Him we are led to do certain things without knowing the reason for doing them. One of those times was about three months before Jerry died. We were talking and I told him that we had been married all those years and he knew all my likes and favorites, but I didn't know his. He asked me what I wanted to know. I asked him what his favorite color was. He replied that it was blue the same as mine. I asked him what his favorite flower was and he replied, yellow roses, same as yours. I asked him what his favorite song was and he replied by wiggling his fingers as if he was playing the piano. He always enjoyed a jazzed up kind of gospel music like our friend, Roy Title, played when he visited while teaching Jerry how to sell family Bibles when Terri was a baby. I believe God prompted that conversation so I would have that information to use in planning Jerry's funeral.

We did as he wanted. Jerry had always been referred to as Nellie's husband because I usually did the talking, but I knew that he was a very special person in his own right and I wanted his funeral service to be one celebrating Jerry's life because he was such a special person. We both knew that God had placed us together and blessed us all of our lives. We met on July 4th weekend, saw each other 3 times over the next 2 months and were married on August 31 and had experienced so many things that could have easily led us apart (separations due to his deployment to Korea twice and Viet Nam, and Germany when we couldn't go with him), financial stress, and medical limitations, and yet we had celebrated 51 anniversaries and were heading towards our 52nd anniversary in just six weeks when he was called home.

Jerry died on July 10, 2004 – exactly 50 years and 3 months after the April 10, 1954 accident that led to his accepting Jesus as his Savior.

Everyone attending Jerry's funeral said it was one of the most joyous celebrations of life they had attended. Pastor Tim spent a lot of time with the family in the few days after Jerry died and he presented the most moving message using scripture from the book of Micah. He specifically used Micah 6: 8 which says,

"He hath showed thee, O man, what is good; and what doth the Lord require of thee, but to do justly, and to love mercy, and to walk humbly with thy God?"

Pastor Tim gave illustrations from Jerry's life that fit into each of the three things required of each of us - to do justly, to love mercy, and to walk humbly with God. We also had comments from my brother who related an incident he observed with Jerry that had taken place several years before.

Gene said, "The whole family was at my parent's home and it was time to go home. Jerry had already gone to the car and was sitting patiently in the driver's seat waiting on Nellie. I told Jerry that he should just drive off and leave Nellie since she was so slow in coming out of the house. Jerry just calmly said, 'She'll come when she gets ready.'"

Gene added that he felt that Jerry was a brother not a brother-in-law.

Our niece asked if she could say something at Uncle Jerry's funeral. I told her she could. I was surprised at her admiration for her Uncle Jerry after her own father had walked out on them. She said Uncle Jerry was what a real father should be and that he was always there for them and anyone who needed help or advice.

In addition we had special music by Roy Tittle – the kind of jazzed up gospel music that Jerry enjoyed. I won't say he loved it because the word *love* was very special to Jerry. He only used it to say " I love God, I love my wife, I love my children and my family". He never used the word love in any other way. He liked other things, but he would never say he loved them. I know that Jerry was pleased with the celebration of his life. He was truly a remarkable, honest, trustworthy, loving person.

I said this was the 10th miracle and it was. The miracle was for Jerry this time. It was determined that he did have cancer and would have had to go through chemotherapy and I believe God knew he was a good, faithful servant, and he had suffered enough so He allowed

The Tenth Miracle - Life without Jerry

Jerry to have the stroke, but gave him 10 days to say goodbye to us before taking him home where he would have a whole body and no more pain or suffering. To me, that is a miracle.

I have been with several friends when they lost their husbands, and I had tried to be there for them. I really didn't understand how they must have felt until I lost Jerry. The physical loss is almost unbearable. Only with God's mercy and strength did I make it through the weeks following his death. Music was something that we shared and Jerry always loved music and would often complain that I had taught so many to play the piano and sing, but I had not taught him. My reply was always the same - you just want to play, you don't want to learn or practice and God didn't give you the natural ability to just sit down and play. Jerry had a wonderful bass voice, but he was tone deaf. He could hear other people's mistakes, especially mine, but he couldn't hear the notes to his own voice so he sang different notes as if they were the same note. He was my helper in every way, especially with music. He worked the sound board for the cantatas and plays that I wrote and directed. He would go over everything with me and help me know what I needed to do to make every project the best it could be.

It was almost a year before I could sit through a church service, particularly the music because that was *our* connection and he was not there to share it with me. God is merciful and He understands our tears and gives us the strength and courage to go on even in our grief. Many nights I fell asleep with my open Bible on my chest reading His words of comfort, knowing that He truly understood my feelings of loneliness. In a way I feel Jesus felt that loneliness the night He was betrayed in the garden. As He prayed for God to lift the burden from Him, but not His will, but Thine be done, His disciples fell asleep leaving Him alone.

Time they say is your friend and as time passes, the pain lessens and the comfort grows.

I continued teaching at college and as I helped the students to grow academically and hopefully spiritually, I began to feel alive again. One of the assignments I give to my students deals with analysis. I ask them to take Robert Frost's poem, "The Road Not Taken" and paraphrase it, then discuss the symbols and finally share some choices they have had to make and how it has affected their life. When reading some of those essays, I fully understood why God had allowed so many different things to take place in my life because it prepared me for what He wanted me to do. While teaching I learn so much about myself and my students and I am able to share some of my experiences that hopefully help them with some things they are dealing with in their own lives.

I am always happy to share my testimony and through the years as a local reporter for our denominations paper, I received many invitations from different churches to share my testimony. The editor of the paper did an article about me and how God had blessed my life with many miracles. With so many students asking me to write my experiences down – write a book – tell your story – I have finally accepted the task to do just that in the hopes that some of the experiences will be inspirational and help others who may be experiencing some of the same things.

Chapter Twelve

The Eleventh Miracle - Learning to Walk again at age 72

"... Daughter, be of good comfort; thy faith hath made thee whole."

Matt. 9:22

At the end of the Spring semester in May, 2008, I went to have outpatient surgery. It seems I had a thyroglocel cist in my throat and it was giving me problems with my speech. My speech had been a challenge ever since the stroke I had at age 38. My larynx was left partially paralyzed which affected my speech. The doctor explained that it was unusual to have it at my age. Usually it was there from birth and would show up before reaching teenage. I was the oldest patient he had ever had that needed surgery. On Friday I had the surgery and had a TIA (mini-stroke) coming out of the anesthesia so they thought I needed to stay in the hospital overnight. An ambulance was called and when the paramedics picked me up, one of them grabbed my left wrist which had an IV in it and mashed it very hard while the other one picked up both ankles and they put me on the gurney to ride to the hospital in the ambulance. When we reached the hospital they picked me up again by my arms and legs and didn't lower the bed rail so my back landed on the bedrail before the bed. I told my daughter that my wrist, leg and back hurt, but the next morning I wanted to go home so they released me.

On Saturday night I tried to walk to the bathroom and it was very painful. My wrist, back and right knee really hurt. Sunday morning I called my daughter and ask her to stop before going to church and bring me Jerry's walker to help me walk as I was in a great deal of pain. She stopped and got the walker for me. She said she would check on me after church. I tried to use the walker but I was in agony. By the time Terri stopped in after church I was in more pain than I had felt in a very long time. She called an ambulance and when I got to the hospital they did a scan on my knee and found that I had bone fragments in my right knee and would have to have emergency total knee replacement. They also x-rayed my back and found that I had a hairline fracture in my pelvis. I don't remember the next few days because they kept me sedated and did not want me to stand on my right leg as it would only create more problems. It would be a couple of days before they could get the surgery scheduled.

While waiting to have the surgery the nurse was putting an IV in my left arm and my left wrist was very painful and I told her that. She said that she was not touching my left wrist. I told her that something was wrong with it. She ordered an x-ray and found that it was broken.

The doctor put a cast on my left wrist.

I had the knee surgery on Thursday of that week and it went well. On Saturday I developed cellulites in both legs. I knew there was a possibility of it because I had bouts of it in the past. The injuries to my legs left me with venus stasis (the blood does not flow back up through my legs to my heart) and that sometimes when the blood pools in my legs it causes cellulites. The major concern was if it settled in the area of the surgery in the knee it could cause me to lose the leg. My doctor called in a specialist and he prescribed several different antibiotics. One of the antibiotics had to be put in intravenously and it would take about an hour for it to finish. About 10 minutes after it started I felt my hand go numb and begin to draw. I told the nurse and she said it wasn't from the antibiotic, but did nothing to help it.

Six hours later they came in to do it again and the same thing happened. I told the nurse that something was happening to my hand, but again, nothing was done as they said I needed the antibiotic or I might lose my leg. I knew something was wrong, but I couldn't get anyone to listen to me. Also the cast had been put on my left wrist too tight and pulled my thumb in an awkward position. I was in so much pain, more than I could ever remember even with the accident and so many injuries. When they came in to repeat the procedure the third time, the same thing happened. Again, nothing was done. It was apparently in my imagination according to them. When they came in to do the fourth time I refused to take it. I honestly would rather lose my leg, or my life than go through that with my hand. As a result, I actually lost some of the use of the nerves in my hand and I have never been able to use it fully since that time. It has affected everything I do with my right hand. I can only grade a few papers at a time and then I have to rest it. I can't pick up a pot or frying pan with that hand.

What started out to be outpatient surgery, led to spending the entire month of May 2008 in the hospital and the next three months with physical therapy, learning to walk again.

In late August I was able to return to teaching. I still needed physical therapy and I had to sit to teach, which is hard for me because I am an active teacher. I hated having to sit and teach. In January, 2009 I was selected as the Outstanding Adjunct Instructor of the Year. On the night the presentation was made the chairperson of the English Department related an incident that had happened during the previous semester.

One of my students had applied to local Cable Company for a position and when she went to the interview the person conducting the interview asked her about her college classes. She told him about her classes and that she was taking English with an exceptional, excellent teacher and that she looked forward to attending class because she not only learned English and improved her writing skills she enjoyed the life experiences shared by her teacher. He asked her for the name of the teacher and she told him it was Mrs. Hartsoe. He asked her if it was Mrs. Nellie Hartsoe and she said it was. He then told her that Mrs. Hartsoe was his teacher when he was in the seventh grade and that she was the reason he went to college and was enjoying his chosen profession.

The chairperson continued by saying Mrs. Hartsoe has been an inspiration to students for a very long time and we are pleased that she is still willing to share her knowledge and experiences with our students here at the college.

My thoughts were that it was ironic that this was my fifth time in my teaching career that I had been selected Teacher of the Year and all of them had been presented on the 10th day of the month. On this particular occasion I felt as if God was saying I had done a good job because at age 18 on April 10, 1954 I had been pronounced Dead on Arrival and God had heard my prayer to extend my life so I could lead Jerry to salvation and here it was at age 74 on January 10, 2009 I was being recognized for using the talent and experiences He had allowed me to have to witness to others. What a wonderful God we have.

Chapter Thirteen

The Twelfth Miracle — Learning to walk again at the age of 76

"Is any sick among you? Let him call for the elders of the church; and let them pray over him, anointing him with oil in the name of the Lord And the prayer of faith shall save the sick, and the Lord shall raise him up; . . ."

James 5:14-15

On Monday evening, July 27, 2011 while working at the computer finalizing grades for my summer school classes, my left knee locked in a bent position and I could not straighten it out. For the few weeks prior to that I knew the knee was getting worse and I had gone to the doctor and he put a shot of cortisone in my knee. He had warned me that it probably wouldn't do any good because it was obvious that the knee needed to be replaced. Due to the terrible time I had when the right knee was replaced I was not anxious to go through that again. Besides the pain I endured at that time, the physical therapy and the time it took to be mobile again I wanted to prolong surgery as long as possible. The fall semester would begin in six weeks and I had already accepted to teach four classes. Recovery with the right knee had taken several months.

My daughter took me to the doctor on Tuesday. I had to go in a wheelchair because I could not walk. He took one look at me and without x-rays he said, "Well, it seems like we've been down this road before. I can't do the surgery Thursday (his regular day for knee replacement surgery) because I already have 5 scheduled, but I'll do yours on Saturday morning." That meant that for the remainder of the week I had to push myself around my house in my computer chair because my bathroom door would not accommodate the wheelchair and I couldn't use a walker. I also had to finish grades.

I figured out that if I had surgery on Saturday, July 30, that I could only stay in the hospital 10 days and then I needed to go home so I could prepare the syllabi needed for my fall classes. I told the doctor he had to have me ready to leave the hospital by August 10 and I would do therapy at home because school was to begin on August 22. He said I would need to have a substitute for the first month of school and I said that would not be fair to the students. He replied that he knew how teachers felt because his mother had taught school for 34 years. He said I would need to work out some way to elevate my leg while in school because it would not good for my leg to leave it in a bent, hanging down position for several hours a day. I told him that my wonderful daughter-in-law had agreed to go to school with me for the first month and be my legs so I wouldn't have to get up and move around.

When I called to pre-register for the surgery the nurse told me I must be very special because my doctor did not do surgery on the weekends and I was the only surgery scheduled for Saturday so I would have undivided attention. I knew that God was working on my behalf and he was answering my prayers that I would be able to continue to meet my teaching obligations.

My surgery was performed on Saturday, July 30 and as before, I began physical therapy in the hospital the next day and by August 12 I went home from the hospital. I could walk a little bit with the use of a walker. I had started work on this book a couple of months before and I knew it would have to be postponed.

I began therapy at home on Monday and the therapist was amazed that I could bend my leg more than required at that time and could walk a little without the walker. I was not surprised because I knew Who was providing my healing. I continued therapy three times a week and I was able to sit at the computer a little while at a time to prepare the syllabi I would need. My youngest son came the week after I came home from the hospital and he was a big help with fixing meals, and helping me email my syllabi to the print shop so the material needed could be printed and ready for the first day of class.

August 22 came and I was prepared for school. As I had told the doctor, Cindy, my wonderful daughter-in-law went with me to school. So you can know how wonderful she really is let me tell you my school schedule. My classes only met on Monday and Wednesday. From 7:00 – 7:55 a.m. I had an English 101 class. From 8:05 – 9:30 a.m. I had an English 102 class followed by another English 102 class from 9:40 – 11:00 a.m. From 11:10 – until 12:45 and from 12:55 - 4:45 I had two Fast Track classes. The Fast Track classes only lasted 4 weeks. After the 4 weeks, I started a 10 week class that consisted of most of the same students I had in Fast Track, but it met from 12:50 until 2:40. This meant that Cindy had to be at my house at 6:30 a.m. to pick me up for the 7 a.m. class because I was not able to drive at that time. She also brought a padded footstool to place under the desk to prop my leg up. She continued to do this for the first month of school.

Since I was back at work the home therapy had to be discontinued and I had to go to a rehab facility for therapy. I felt God's help in my recovery. It was difficult and painful, but I didn't develop cellulites and the healing process was going so much faster than recovery from the right knee surgery. By the end of August I was able to drive and go to school and Cindy was not required to go with me anymore. She said she really missed it and had gotten to know some of the students and she would ask me about some of them as the semester went on.

Walking was difficult, but God had worked another miracle and allowed me to do something in half the time it had taken with the right knee. Now I'm not going to tell you that everything was easy. There was a lot of pain and six weeks after the surgery I did develop cellulites and had to take two rounds of antibiotics, but it did not clear up the cellulites. The only thing I could do was to wear the support hose, and try to elevate my legs several hours a day to try to relieve the swelling. I also had to put ice on my knee for two hours at a time.

Once again God had performed a miracle and allowed me to learn to walk again without assistance. God always knows what we need without our asking Him, but He still wants us to ask Him for guidance. I think it is a blessing that we can talk to Him and He understands our needs. He places people in our path that make it possible for us to receive blessings that become the miracles in our lives. What an awesome God we have that treats us like we are the only special person in His life. He loves us unconditionally and sent His only Son to die on a cross becoming the perfect Lamb sacrificed making it possible to be forgiven and have eternal life. It is so amazing that the only thing He asks from us is to love Him as He loves us, praise His name and allow Him to live in our hearts guiding and directing our paths. He also sent the Holy Spirit to be with us so we would never be alone.

Chapter Fourteen

The Story continues

"Then shall the King say unto them on his right hand, Come, ye blessed of my Father, inherit the kingdom prepared for you from the foundation of the world."

Matthew 25:24

Towards the end of September, the chairperson of the English department asked for someone to teach an English 102 class as the instructor had to be out on medical leave the rest of the semester. Since the time fit between my 11:00 am and 12:45 class and I was already teaching two English 102 classes I thought I would be able to help out so I called and accepted the class. After I accepted the class I found out that the instructor of that class was using a different textbook than I was using so it meant that I would have to develop a completely new syllabus and because the instructor had been absent a great deal it was difficult to know where to begin and what to use from what the students had already covered.

The Story continues

During this same time my mother, who had been in a nursing home for five years, was failing in health. The doctor and I had discussed bringing in hospice. I went to see mother on Thursday morning, September 29. I could tell she was not doing well. I read the Bible to her and we sang some songs. Mother still knew the words to "What a Friend we have in Jesus", "Jesus Loves Me" and "The Old Rugged Cross". That morning the care giver was in her room and said she had been taking care of her the past three weeks and she was much weaker now than when she first started taking care of her. The past couple of weeks she had not talked above a whisper and for the past year she would only eat pudding and all her food had to be minced because the scan they did on her throat showed that her esophagus had deteriorated due to arthritis and aging. She had great difficulty swallowing her food. The doctor said it would not get better. She had lost a great deal of weight. I called my sister that afternoon and told her I thought mother was worse and that the doctor and I had decided to call in hospice. The doctor called me on Friday evening, September 30 and said he was writing the order for hospice but it would probably be Monday before they could be contacted. On Saturday, my sister, Faye, her son and daughter-in-law and their son and their daughter and her baby went to visit mother. Faye called me when they got home and said she didn't think mother knew them and the only time she responded was when she looked at the baby, Lily, and smiled. She said she was so concerned that she planned to go back and spend some time with Mother on Sunday.

My sister has a lot of medical problems and has to have oxygen so it is difficult for her to go. I knew for her to go she must be really concerned about Mother.

Late Sunday evening Faye called me and said she had just left mother. She said Mother's breathing was very labored. She said Mother told her she felt like she was constipated. Faye said she told the nurse and the nurse said she couldn't give her a laxative without an order from the doctor. The nurse said there was something she could give her that might help. Immediately after mother drank what the nurse gave her she vomited. Faye stayed until Mother's breathing eased off and she fell asleep. Faye said she was worried about her. Sunday night the doctor called and told me that Mother was resting peacefully and assured me that he had written the order for hospice and put it under the social worker's door to start the process for hospice Monday morning. He also said he had ordered an x-ray for Mother's chest to see if she had retained anything from vomiting earlier that day.

On Monday, after classes, I had a message from the nursing home. I called and the receptionist said she didn't know who had called but she would connect me to the nurse's station on hall 100. When the person answered the phone I asked if someone had called me and she said she would ask the nurse. I heard her ask the nurse if someone had called Ms. Walter's daughter and the nurse said she had not called. I asked the person on the phone how my mother was and she replied, "Oh, she is just fine." I told her to tell mother I would see

The Story continues

her in the morning. The date was Oct. 3 which is also my brother's birthday. The time was about 2:30 when I talked to the nursing home. I called my brother and sang happy birthday to him. After hanging up from him I thought that maybe the social worker had called me about setting up hospice. I called the nursing home back and asked to speak to the social worker. When she answered the phone she said she had called me and that we could not use the hospice that we had requested and that administration had said we would have to use one of the three hospice groups the nursing home had under contract.

I had told the head nurse and the social worker at the last care meeting I attended three weeks earlier that I was not satisfied with the care mother was receiving. I reminded the social worker of my discontent with her care and asked her how I was expected to trust someone I had no connection to with mother's care and I didn't understand why we could not use the hospice group we had requested. She promptly said, "Would you like me to help you find another facility for Ms. Walters?" That made me angry and I felt like telling her yes, but I knew mother was too weak to be moved and I told her that I felt that moving mother at this time would be detrimental to her and to give me the names of the hospice groups and I would call and talk with them and see if I felt I could trust them to care for mother. She gave me the names and I told her that if I couldn't have confidence in any of the three that I would come and talk with administration to find out why we could not have the hospice group we wanted.

I was very tired and my legs hurt because that was also the day I started the new class I was taking from the teacher who had to go out on medical leave. I was still recovering from knee surgery. I sat down in the recliner and elevated my legs to try and relieve the pain and reduce the swelling. I fell asleep. The phone woke me up. It was 4:15 and it was the nursing home. The person on the phone identified herself and then asked if I could come to the facility. I asked her why, what was wrong and she replied she would tell me when I got there. I asked if my mother was o.k. She hesitated and then said, "Well, No." I told her I was on my way. I had a very uneasy feeling.

I called my sister and told her they had called me to come to the nursing home. I asked if she wanted to go with me and she said she wanted to go. I also called my daughter and told her if she tried to call me I would not be home because they had called from the nursing home and I felt something was wrong and they didn't tell me anything and I was picking up Aunt Faye and Robin. The reason I called my daughter was so she wouldn't be upset if she didn't get me on the phone. She always called when she got off from work and we would chat until she either arrived home or where ever she might be going.

My daughter works half way from home to the nursing home. She left work and went to the nursing home arriving there around 4:40. I picked up my sister and her daughter and we arrived at the nursing home about 5 p.m. It takes 30 minutes to go from my house to the nursing home and my sister lives on the way about 5 miles from my home. My daughter, Terri, met us in the parking area and whispered

The Story continues

to me that she thought grandmother had died. She said when she got there grandmother's door was closed and they would not let her go in. She asked why she couldn't go in and was told that they were cleaning her up.

We entered the facility, walked past the nurses' station to Mother's room. No one said anything to us and the nurse was at the station. Mother's door was closed and I opened it and was shocked at what I saw. My mother was in bed on her back and her eyes were half open, her mouth was wide open and she had an oxygen tube in her nose with the oxygen still running. I walked over to the bed and kissed her fore-head and it was cold. I closed her mouth and eyes. I took the oxygen out of her nose. It was strange that she was dead, but she still had oxygen going into her nose. My daughter went to the nurse's desk and asked when her grandmother had died. The nurse didn't answer her and would not give her any information about when they put her on oxygen. She asked if Mother had been on oxygen all day. She asked why I was told at 2:30 that she was fine. She did not get any answers. An hour later no one had come to talk with us or give us any information. Terri went to the nurse's desk and asked the nurse again when her grandmother had died and the cause of death. The nurse finally said she died at 4:45 p.m. My daughter realized that was the time she tried to enter her grandmother's room and was told she couldn't go in that they were cleaning her up. At 6 p.m. I called my brother whom I had sung happy birthday to a few hours earlier and told him that mother had passed away. He replied, "Boy, that's not a good birthday present."

My sister and I never left mother's room from 5 p.m. until 7 p.m. when the undertaker and the doctor came in at the same time. My daughter had asked the nurse to call the funeral home (we had actually made arrangements with the funeral home almost a year before because mother had a bad spell and we weren't sure she would live until Thanksgiving or Christmas, but she surprised us. After they gave her two pints of blood she made it through Thanksgiving, Christmas and her 96th birthday in July), Terri also heard the nurse call the coroner and tell them that mother had died. It seems that if a person dies in a nursing home the coroner does not have to come to verify the death.

While we were waiting for someone to talk to us or check on us to see if we needed something or not, Robin and Terri began packing up grandmother's clothes and things to take home. At seven o'clock when the doctor came in I was standing at the end of mother's bed and my sister was sitting beside mother. The doctor walked to me, put his hand on my shoulder and said, "Well, I guess she was sicker than we knew. Her kidneys just stopped functioning." I wanted to say, "We knew it and tried to tell you and this facility, but I believe you felt she was too old to care about and needed to die." We left shortly after 7 p.m. and no one from the facility offered us any help, assistance, or condolences during the time we were there and three weeks after mother died the nursing home sent a new King James Bible and it was endorsed

To Mrs. Janie Kennedy Walters

With sympathy and signed the facilities name.

The Story continues

The death certificate stated that the time of death was 4:45 and the cause of death was Acute Renal Failure.

There are so many unanswered questions surrounding mother's death. We do know where she is. Without any doubt we know that she is safe in the arms of Jesus. She served Him a long time. On one occasion I was sharing an obituary from the newspaper and I asked mother what she would like for people to remember about her and she thought for a long time and finally said, "I want them to say that I lived a long time and helped people." The Bible states that Jesus said, "… Verily I say unto you, inasmuch as ye have done it unto one of the least of these my brethren, ye have done it unto me." That was true for our mother. Mother had made her own preparation for her funeral in 1999 and wrote it down in her own handwriting. She gave her directions and the clothes she wanted to be buried in to my sister. She revised a little of it a couple of years later. She wanted her grandchildren to serve as pallbearers and she wrote the following note in her own handwriting:

My wonderful Mother

I love you all and please be happy for me. I have suffered a long time.

All of you just please live where you will come be with your daddy and me and with Jesus, where there will be no more pain and sorrow. Won't that be wonderful. All my love to my children, in-laws, grands and great-grands and their spouses and great-great grands. I love you all, Mother, Grandmother, Great-Grandmother, Great, Great grandmother and Friend to all.

These words from my mother reflects what a wonderful example my mother set for my family. Her love of family and God was present in everything she did. I have tried to set the same kind of examples in my own family. My son-in-law, Tom, wrote me a letter for Mother's Day in 2005, the year after my husband went home to be with the Lord. I hope his words will be an inspiration to you who read this book. With all the mother-in-law jokes that give a negative view of this position, I hope you will be encouraged by his words. They are very special to me. I love you, Tom. Terri and Tom have been married 31 years.

Mothers

God created Mothers because He knew that the world He created could not survive without the special qualities that He gave them. Without Mothers, we would have no way to enter this world. The labor that Mother's endure throughout the birth process is just the beginning.

A Mother's task just starts with birth. From that time on

The Story continues

she must nurture, teach, discipline, clothe and shelter her children. From a Mother, her children learn right from wrong and a good Mother teaches her children about God and His miracles and His Son, who was born to give all of us eternal life.

Mother-in-laws are special people as well. They entrust their children to another person to live with and to go out into the world in order to make their own lives. You think that it's just a joke when I say that you are my favorite Mother-in-Law, but it's true. You see, I've had two others with whom to compare. You are without a doubt the best, therefore my favorite.

On this Mother's Day, I commend you on the way you sought to raise your daughter, my wife. I thank you for bringing her into the world and teaching her the values that she has today. You have always known that she was special, and so do I. She is my life.

Have a Happy Mother's Day, Mom. I love you, Tom

I entitled this chapter, The Story Continues for a reason. I do not know what the future holds for me, but I do know who holds the future in His loving hands.

For many years I have treasured my out of body experience and I would do it all over again because I was able to have a glimpse of heaven and feel God's powerful love and know how much He loves me. He heard my plea and granted my prayer to let me live. I didn't specify how long only that I wanted enough time to lead Jerry to salvation and that took place within three weeks after the accident. That was 58 years ago and He gave me 50 of those with Jerry. Every time I gave my testimony and shared my out of body experience people would respond with you need to write a book. The reason it has taken me so long is because it is so special to me that Jesus loves me so much that he has given me many more miracles that I could write another book, but I have tried to share the miracles that I felt would help others who may have to face some of the same situations. I want everyone to know that God is with us and that He understands and will never leave us.

I am looking forward to the next opportunities that God will allow me to experience. That's why the story will continue until I finish what God has for me to do and He will take me home to be with Him, Jerry

and the rest of my family that have made that final journey and are safe in the arms of God.

My favorite verse of scripture helps me day by day. I hope it will help you, too.

"But seek ye first the kingdom of God,
and his righteousness;
and all these things shall be added unto you.
Take therefore no thought for the morrow:

for the morrow shall take thought for the things of itself. Sufficient unto the day is the evil thereof.

Matthew 6:33-34

Comments from my family

My three precious children, gifts from God

Jerry, Jr. Steven, Terri (taken in 1993)

As the oldest, I knew a lot of what is in my mother's book, but there is a lot that I did not know. She is a remarkable woman to say the least with everything she has been through. I truly believe God gave her life back to her to make a difference, not only in my dad's life, but in so many other lives. She has been an inspirational example to many people through her music, teaching, and youth ministries. This shows very much in Columbia, SC. She can't go anywhere without someone she has taught coming up to her and telling her what a difference she made in their life. Reading this book will be a blessing to you and make a difference in your life.

Jerry E. Hartsoe, Jr. (Buzzy)

This book is a long fulfilled dream of mine and my son, James. We have badgered Moma to tell her story of courage and unwavering faith for many years. It was ironic that she called me to read the book for her and be critical because all through college that's what I had asked her to do to all the papers I had to write and rewrite. While she was writing this book, we had some lively conversations, shed some tears, and laughed a lot going through memories and pictures. I know that writing parts of this book was very hard for her – to relive and re-visit the times and things she has gone through. I have asked her and Daddy over the years – "Aren't you mad at the guy that hit you and changed your lives so drastically?" Their answer was always the same – why should we be mad – we've had a good life – God has taken care of us, and that was that. Moma never hesitates to share her testimony in whatever way she can and she doesn't just talk about it she lives it. She has been lucky enough to find her true calling in teaching music and academics and through that she has been able to touch so many lives and encourage so many to never give up. She doesn't give mixed signals – she doesn't waiver in her beliefs and by doing so she was the best example that we kids could have. She is my rock. Thanks, Moma, I love you and I've always been proud to be your daughter!

Terri Lynn Hartsoe Whitehead

The Story continues

My Mom has been the strongest Godly influence in my life. Whenever I was going through my highest of highs and lowest of lows, my Mom would always point me to God. I would absolutely not be the Man I am today without my Mom playing a very big part in it. If I have something needing prayers, whether it's for me or someone else, I always call my Mom for her help. You see, I believe because of my Mom's accident long before I was born, she has a direct link to God when she goes to Him in prayer. I only hope that as I mature in life, I have the same love for God that my Mom has and has tried to share with me. I grew up knowing that my Mom was a special person, but until reading this book, even I didn't know just how special. There are stories in this book that I knew and ones that I read for the first time. Like my sister told me she had, I, too, had times where I laughed out loud and times that I wept. Thank you Mom for all you have done for me and continue to do. Thank you God for letting my Mom live and spread Your love to everyone her life has touched.

Steven Michael Hartsoe

Faye, my wonderful sister's comments

When my sister, Nellie, asked me to read and comment on her book I was very honored. My sister is a woman of many words and I am a woman with very few words. In reading Nellie's book about the many events in her life I noticed one thing that was always there, the love she has for her family and the greater love she has for her Lord and Savior. I know that everyone who takes time to read this book will come away with a sense of encouragement and faith that walking with Jesus every day we can all have. We can make a difference in others lives.

I was there when the hospital called and told us that Nellie had died. I was there in the hospital when the doctor's told us that God had sent an angel to let them know that Nellie was alive and she was in surgery fighting to survive. We faced a great loss that day and then a great joy that God still had work for Nellie to do on this earth. This book does not tell all the things she has done in her life to glorify our Lord. Let me just say, for me, the love of life and her joy in Jesus has always helped me to not give up, but to keep going. Thank you, Nellie, for being my sister and my friend. I love you.

Carolyn Faye Kennedy Seyle

Karen, my talented sister-in-law's comments

Nellie's life is truly a miracle-filled life! I'm not just talking about the little everyday type miracles that we can all claim if we truly thought about it. I'm talking <u>**MAJOR MIRACLES!**</u>

One's whole life can change in a blink of an eye and sometimes . . .many times, there is no going back. However, on April 10, 1954, Nellie was brought back . . .to serve as a Blessing and inspiration to her husband, family, friends, as well as the hundreds of students over decades of teaching and whom she continues to inspire daily. This is her special story. After hearing bits and pieces of it over the course of 30+ years, I am so pleased that she is finally sharing it, and her walk with Christ, for all to read.

Karen Jeglum Kennedy

My brothers and sister on our trip to the mountains October, 2012

Includes left to right –
Mary Lou, Leroy, Jr., Faye, Nellie, Gene

Twelve Miracles Including a Glimpse of Heaven

Partial List of Recognitions and Awards
for Nellie Kennedy Hartsoe

Listed in 1968 Outstanding Young Women in America

1969 Nominated for Outstanding Military Wife of the Year

1969 President of PWOC – Crailsheim, Germany

1969 – Writer and Director of Easter Contata – A Promise Fulfilled – Crailsheim, Germany

1985-86 Teacher of the Year – Caughman Road Middle School

1989 – Teacher of the Year – Atlas Road Alternative School

1988-89 - Teacher of the Year - Southern Technical College

1990 - Teacher of the Year – Department of Juvenile Justice

1990 – Recipient of $20,000 grant from SC Arts Commission for Music/Drama – DJJ

The Story continues

1991 – Recipient of $20,000 grant from SC Arts Commission for Music/Drama – DJJ

1994 – Certificate of Appreciation – Birchwood High School - DJJ

1995 – Played the role of Mrs. DuBose in "To Kill a Mockingbird" - The Playhouse

Family Theatre

1996 – First place Certificate – Short Stories – Southeastern Writer's Conference

1996 – First place Certificate – Play Writing – Southeastern Writer's Conference

1997 – Recipient of Award for Music Director – Southside Baptist Church

2009 – Outstanding Adjunct Instructor – Midlands Technical College

In addition she has written, directed and performed in many plays, participated in

Creative Ministries Programs as Director, performer, and instructor.

She also holds a Master of Education – Curriculum from the University of South Carolina

CPSIA information can be obtained at www.ICGtesting.com
Printed in the USA
BVOW08s0913141015

422396BV00002B/167/P